ESSAYS
IN APPRECIATION

BERNARD BERENSON

ESSAYS
IN APPRECIATION

38517

1958

CHAPMAN & HALL
LONDON

© BERNARD BERENSON 1958

Printed in Great Britain by Butler & Tanner Ltd., Frome & London

CAT. NO. 4189/4

TO THE MEMORY OF
ARTURO LORIA

ACKNOWLEDGMENTS
(Illustrations)

AGENZIA FOTOGRAFICA INTERNAZIONALE, VENICE : 67.
ALINARI, FLORENCE : 3, 4, 19, 32, 48, 75, 76, 101, 102, 103.
ANDERSON, ROME : 33, 63, 68, 71, 74, 77, 78, 105, 109.
ARTI GRAFICHE, BERGAMO : 61. BOCCARDI C., ROME : 87,
88. BRAUN, MULHOUSE-DORNACH : 17. BRITISH MUSEUM,
LONDON : 5, 6, 7, 8, 9, 11. CLEVELAND MUSEUM OF ART,
OHIO : 41, 44. CONDAKS STUDIOS, PHILADELPHIA : 52.
A. C. COOPER, F.R.P.S., LONDON : 69. DAINESI, MILAN : 49.
ELECTA EDITRICE, MILAN (GRASSI) : 23, 64, 99. FIORENTINI,
VENICE : 27, 29, 30, 47, 65, 66, 90, 91, 92. FOTOTECA
BERENSON : 1, 10, 12, 14, 15, 20, 21, 22, 24, 26, 28, 31,
34, 35, 36, 37, 42, 45, 51, 54, 55, 57, 58, 59, 60, 62, 70, 72,
79, 80, 81, 82, 84, 85, 86, 89, 93, 94, 95, 96, 97 a & b,
106, 108. GABINETTO FOTOGRAFICO SOVRINTENDENZA ALLE
GALLERIE, FLORENCE : 13, 98, 100, 104, 107. GIRAUDON,
PARIS : 38. GRAY, E. WILLIAM, LONDON : 83. ISTITUTO
ITALIANO ARTI GRAFICHE, BERGAMO : 16. LABORATORIO
RICERCHE SCIENTIFICHE PINACOTECA DI BRERA, MILAN : 50.
MUSEUM OF FINE ARTS, BOSTON (MASS.) : 2. NATIONAL
GALLERY, DUBLIN : 25. NATIONAL GALLERY, LONDON : 69.
NATIONAL GALLERY OF ART, WASHINGTON (KRESS COLLEC-
TION) : 40, 43. PHOTO CHEVOYON, PARIS : 53, 56. REALI
A., FLORENCE : 39. STAATLISCHE PHOTOTHEK, DRESDEN : 46.
VILLANI, BOLOGNA : 110, 111, 112, 113, 114, 115, 116, 117.
WALTER ART GALLERY, BALTIMORE : 18.

ACKNOWLEDGMENTS

Acknowledgment is made to the Editors of the following publications in which the essays have appeared :

Arte Veneta : Number 14

Beiträge für Georg Swarzenski : Number 3

Burlington Magazine : Number 4

Corriere della Sera : Numbers 8, 9, 10, 11, 12, 13, 15, 18, 19, 20

Esposizione dell' Arte Tessile e della Moda : Number 5

Illustrazione Italiana : Number 7

New Statesman and Nation : Number 2

Ponte : Number 1

Revue des Arts : Number 6

Rivista d'Arte : Number 3

Rivista della Biennale : Number 17

Scritti in onore di Lionello Venturi : Number 16

CONTENTS

x

I

ON THE RECONSTRUCTION OF FLORENCE

The picturesque is an epithet applied to what man builds instinctively, as the bee its hive, the bird its nest, the beaver its dam. If it happens either that the conglomerate of edifices put up with no thought of architecture turns out, seen close at hand, to have a harmony of its own, that it adorns a hillside in the middle distance or enriches a curve of the horizon, we designate it, if we are careful with words, not as beautiful but as picturesque.

We reserve the word " architectural " for structures that are not mere building. Mere building has no more claim to be architecture than mere carpentry or stone-cutting has of being sculpture, or the brushing of pigments on doors, windows, tables, chairs, etc. etc., of being the art of painters like Titian or Turner. Architecture employs building to carry out its deliberately planned and elaborated ideas—ideas of environment, of material, of dimension, of proportion, of bulk, of relief, of light and shade, never of utility alone. Indeed a great Renaissance architect like Leon Battista Alberti almost disclaimed the builder and would not himself carry out an edifice he designed.

A few examples may help to make my meaning clear. Thus we never think of the Acropolis of Athens as picturesque, nor even of the Roman Capitol. Supremely picturesque was the Florentine Mercato Vecchio with its approaches and exits, its delicate colonnades contrasting with the cliff-like pile of the Ghetto towering over it (Plate 1). Picturesque is the great Piazza of Siena but not the Piazza of St. Peter or San Marco. Picturesque is many a market square in Central Europe but not the Place de la Concorde in Paris or the Place Stanislas at Nancy. Romantically picturesque are ruins not only in a desolate landscape but in the heart of a city, as to our cost we see in our own, picturesque enough to inspire a nostalgic wish to leave them untouched.

So much to the extent of our purpose for the picturesque and the architectural. There remains a third type of structure to which neither the categories, picturesqueness or architecturalness, need apply. It is a tower. It can be architectural as the Campanile of San Marco, or of Cremona, or of Giotto at Florence—this last indeed almost beyond architecture and on the way to jewellery, like the exquisitely carved pedestal by Cellini for his Perseus. It can be impressive like the Hohenstaufen castle at San Miniato al Tedesco. In company with others it can be poetically picturesque on a hill distant enough to fuse with the landscape. Seen on level ground at close range, huddled together like tall tombstones in a crowded cemetery, towers are quaint, even when not absurd like the Asinelli at Bologna that lean as if in a drunken embrace. " Quaint " is the epithet one should apply to edifices that are neither architectural nor picturesque, but odd, queer, unassimilable, yet not altogether unattractive.

Having these categories in mind, the architectural, the picturesque and the quaint, we shall not encounter great difficulties in deciding what we should like to do with the part of Florence destroyed by the Wehrmacht.

In the first place we must ask whether we want

to restore it, or to use it as land for building. If the latter is our purpose, there is nothing to be said except that it would be cheaper to leave the ruins to their romantic future and to move the centre of the city away from the Arno into the plain.

If on the other hand we care for Florence as the historical entity it has been for centuries, an aspect of shapes and profiles singularly unaltered despite the changes to which the habitations of man are subject, then, in the words used in connection with the collapsed tower of San Marco, it must be replaced " where it was and as it was ".

The objection may be raised that it is not so simple a problem to resolve a complex like the Florence of Por' Santa Maria and what lies between Ponte Vecchio and Ponte Santa Trinita as to rebuild the Venetian *Campanile*. The latter presented an ultra rational problem of architectural reconstruction : the former, on the contrary, the problem of reproducing the picturesque, of using stone and wood and iron and plaster and wash to paint on a scale of nature so many pictures by Francesco Guardi.

Yet if we want to do it we can do it. There is an abundance of drawings, engravings, etchings, photographs, water-colours and other visual documents for the purpose. All that is wanted is the goodwill, the hearty determination to carry it through (Plate 2).

Other ideas are not lacking. I hope the one rife some decades ago will not return. It came in the wake of the Vandal cyclone that threw down the walls of the city, and swept away Mercato Vecchio, while many advocated demolishing Ponte Vecchio and replacing it with a flat and commodious bridge satisfying the demands of to-day's traffic. They wanted to clear away the wedge of buildings between the bridges and San Felice in Piazza to turn the space thus gained into a public garden with the usual accompaniment of faded grass, sickly geraniums, consumptive palm trees, as well as benches and lanterns painted green, etc.

The danger just now is that some may advocate clearing away the ruins on the Arno between the two bridges and permanently exposing to view the remaining front of Borgo San Jacopo almost untouched by the Nazi blasts.

To this I have serious objections. In the first place this front is too grimly, too frowningly medieval to face across the river another façade of character so gay, so mixed, and on the whole of such XVIIIth-century aspect. (Plate 4.) The contrast would be too violent.

There remains an even more cogent reason for discarding it. It is that for centuries when the word " Florence " was spoken or read, the visual image that first flashed on the mind was of the Ponte Vecchio and the opposite side of the Arno as one saw it while walking along the Lungarno Acciaioli (Plate 3). Other mental pictures followed on reflection, but as extensions and as detail : the Cathedral, the Baptistery, Piazza della Signoria, this or that square, church or palace. They completed, filled out, but did not alter the first spontaneous evocation. Failure to restore it would be to replace the memory picture of the Florence we and our forerunners have known for generation after generation with something that broke with the past so violently that at first glance we could not recognize the identity and should have to reconstruct it by piecing together this and that wisp of visual recollection. That may leave indifferent the utilitarian denizens but scarcely the citizen acquainted with his city's past, aware of what its traditional aspect means to him. Still more may it mean to the outsider, who, just because he has no workaday connection with it, can contemplate it as an exhalation of sheer beauty, expressing the taste of people artistically more sensitive than any other that Europe has known in the last 2,000 years.

Surely it would be possible for each proprietor to do what he pleased with the interior of his house, arrange spaces and staircases to his taste or convenience and to put in all up-to-date improvements. This has been done all over Europe with buildings that have not altered their outer aspect and yet, as I know by having frequented them, have been made as liveable as any freshly-put-up house of to-day.

So much for the Oltrarno. I should propose dealing in the same way with Por' Santa Maria and the ruined part of Lungarno Acciajuoli. What lies behind them does not form part of the spontaneous evocation just mentioned and can be treated according to the value each building or group of buildings had for its picturesque character or its architectural beauty. I would severely avoid demolitions that would expose isolated towers, which at best would look but quaint.

Our Florence, the Florence of the ripe Renaissance, Baroque, and Rococo, is anything but quaint. The numerous towers that, like other towns, it had in the Middle Ages, were with rare exceptions so incorporated into structures with a

E.A.—B

relatively uniform sky-line as to lose not only their prominence but even their identity. To isolate this or that one and thereby draw attention to it would be to introduce as inharmonious a note as would be a merely utilitarian edifice, a *machine à vivre*, or an up-to-date office building.

The Florence that we know as a work of art would remain a fragment without the Ponte Santa Trinita. No doubt there are great difficulties in restoring a structure of curves so subtle, of mouldings so delicate, of a patina so ivory-like. I venture to assert that here too it is a question of goodwill and patience.

At first and for some years it will not satisfy perfectionists. It will look a bit raw and the curves a trifle too geometrical. But so has every structure looked until time has caressed and licked away its asperities and relaxed the rigidity of its outlines. Perfectionists fail to consider this and consequently oppose all attempts at restoration. They thereby play into the hands of those who prefer the entirely new.

In detail Naples and Palermo have suffered more than Florence, but apparently not in a way to threaten reconstruction that would alter the traditional aspect of either. The first great town where this danger exists is Florence, and what is done here, for no better reason than that it offers a model to imitate, may be followed by many other towns in the North. On that account alone we must be doubly aware of what we are doing here.

There remains an even more cogent reason. It is that Florence has a responsibility to the rest of Italy, and perhaps to the European world in every part of the globe owing to an indisputable fact in art history. It is a fact that wherever European influence goes, it takes not only to all the Americas but to India, to China, to Japan, an architecture, no matter how developed and trans-formed by more recent and latest requirements, an architecture and urban landscape that were worked out by Florentines and their pupils from elsewhere in the XVth and XVIth centuries. In no other art has Florence influenced the world so much, not even in painting or in sculpture.

This fact gives Florence an authority still felt everywhere in Italy and beyond, and with this a responsibility of which it cannot divest itself.

I Tatti
Settignano
March 1945

II

PAINTING AND NATIONAL INCOME

" England must export." Corollary, she should export goods on which the greatest profit is to be made. At the present moment there is no item of export on which as much profit is to be made as paintings. A picture by an accredited master fetches a price that has scarcely any economic relation to the cost of the raw materials required—a bit of canvas, a tube of paint, a stretcher—or of the labour hours employed by the painter, his models and servants, or of his rent, heating and lighting. The profit may range up to thousands of times the outlay.

It is not enough that the artist should be accredited at home, that he should be highly thought of, discussed, disparaged and wrangled over in the studios of Chelsea, St. John's Wood and Bloomsbury. His reputation must cross frontiers and oceans, must dart over Germany to Uzbekistan and across Atlantics and Pacifics to empires and dominions overseas. Then and only then do the products of his workshop become a national asset and he a goose laying golden eggs.

It is too late to tap this matchless source of profit during the present crisis, but in expectation of the next war, government should lose no time in starting schools of painting and accompany them with schools of advertisers. They should be made a national concern as they have been in France for all but three centuries. The harvest that France has reaped, and is still reaping, owing to this early sowing, must stand it in good stead in this hour of need.

At this point someone may ask about the Old Masters still adorning the stately homes of England. To begin with, few of these homes retain the works of art their occupants brought back from grand tours, or had done by the great portraitists of the decades before and after 1800. Moreover, to the extent that they still are in England, they are in the nature of capital and not of income.

It would be interesting to know what the export of contemporary paintings—not of " Old Masters "—has added to the income of the French people during the last eighty years, that is to say ever since there started a demand, first in the United States and then elsewhere, for Millet and other artists of the Barbizon School, then for Manet and the so-called "Impressionists", followed by the galaxy of genius still producing masterpieces for which fabulous prices are being paid.

This demand is based on real merit. French painting for the decades following 1860 has been as universalized as French so-called " Gothic " art of every kind was in the XIIth, XIIIth and XIVth centuries. England alone held out but only to the end of the XIXth century. Since then native sources have run dry and English painting, like painting elsewhere in the white man's world, is watered by springs that bubble up in Paris. Russian and Italian, German and American, Scandinavian and Spanish still seem to enjoy a certain independence. When you look close, you see that it is chiefly a matter of local colour and costume in the subject matter. In all that is essential, they are as French as any Frenchman of the same competence ; and we must not be taken in by what seems originality and is only incompetence.

None the less merit alone would not account for the spread of French painting the world over.

There is the fact of Paris as the most attractive
gathering-place in the white man's world. The
artist in whatever art, be it visual, verbal or
auricular, the thinker, the scientist, the scholar,
all can learn something there or—more important
—be stimulated and given zest for learning.
This holds more for the painter than for others.
The painter finds there not only academic studios,
teachers and masters, but fellow-students from
every corner of the world, who come there not
as one goes to school in a routine way, but as to
the most marvellous of all adventures, where, if
ever, he will live intensely and realize himself
completely. What would have become of a
Whistler had he stuck to his native Baltimore, or
of a Sargent at Philadelphia, of a Boldini at
Ferrara, of a Modigliani at Leghorn, of a Sert
at Barcelona or of a Picasso at Valencia ? Local
celebrities no doubt and nothing more.

Some of the most successful—nearly all those
just mentioned—remain in Paris for the rest of
their days and their immense earnings increase
the national wealth of France. Most return to
their own countries or drift to where they thrive.
Wherever they go, they go as advertisers of contemporary French painting. That is spontaneous
and the more so as the returned native at

Czernowitz, Bucarest, Berlin, Madrid, Philadelphia and even New York looks back with
increasingly nostalgic glamour to the months or
years he spent as an aspirant in Paris.

Not quite so spontaneous, although I have
never been able to discover any trace of deliberately organized propaganda, is the attitude in
Paris of the government organs, of the Press, of
the public, of society, of men of letters and above
all of the trade. Nowhere on earth is the
emergent artist of promise favoured and his
success applauded as much as in Paris. The
journalists and dealers cannot do enough to praise
the favourite, to explain him, to evaluate him,
to boom him. Visiting critics are roped in,
dined and wined until their eyes are opened to
see what they are wanted to see. One almost
suspects organization of some sort, in the nature,
say, of what one feels but scarcely sees in the
mass-enthusiasm accompanying processions at
Lourdes. Look at the results. The English
people by their authoritative art organization are
invited, commanded almost, to take train from
anywhere between John o' Groat's and Land's
End to see and worship the works of the most
successful of these Parisian painters. Quarrels
ensue, threatening to be as serious as those over

theological questions at Alexandria and Constantinople, and nothing advertises like fierce dis-
putes. In Sioux City, in Wally Wally, in Tomb-
stone and many other American cities courses on
Picasso are announced and students—female
mostly—are encouraged " to major " in them.
(I do not quite know what it means, to " major ".
Presumably it is something nice.)

What can English painters do to get as talked
about, as appreciated, as written about, as discussed and, above all, to get as well paid as the
Parisian painters whom the English public so
generously and so suicidally does so much to
advertise ? Remember that England still remains
the lawgiver to its cousins overseas and that its
enthusiasms are loudly echoed by them.

Can nothing be done to turn some channels of
the golden Mississippi into the Thames without
diminishing the Seine ?

The Victorian era seems to have impoverished
the English genius for painting as much as the
XVIIth-century puritanical reaction impoverished drama and music. Surely the England
that produced the galaxy of portraitists ending
with Lawrence, and landscapists dying in beauty
with Constable and Turner, are not physio-
psychologically unfitted to paint. The reason

for the decline in pictorial genius cannot be constitutional and must be relatively superficial.

First and last the English must get over their inferiority complex, which drives them at the same time to deny their present incompetence and to despair over it.

They must not doubt their innate gifts, their superiority to most Europeans in conveying, not only verbally but visually, a sense of the fanciful, the imaginative, the romantic. The now-so-despised Victorians had a Burne-Jones, a creator of wistfulness, and in Watts an allegorist who leaves out of sight Frenchmen like Gustave Moreau, still greatly admired by many painters and many critics among his own people. Can we wonder that others take the English at the valuation of their lion-whelps and jackals? They must recover a well-considered conceit of themselves.

They must learn to draw. How long does it take a medical student to get his degree? Six, seven, eight years before he is allowed to practice. How many youngsters are ready to work as hard learning to draw? Yet drawing is as difficult and takes as long a training and without it the painter is only the kind of practitioner that the doctor is who has but a fake degree.

Nor can he begin soon enough. It is too late

if he starts as a Cambridge or Oxford graduate, and besides, by that time he has learned too well how to express himself with words to feel the imperative need, even if he reached the ability, to express himself in visual form. The university graduate turned painter seldom acquires more than an over-absorbing interest in the " secret of the Old Masters " and an insatiable lust for tempera painting. In his own pictures he scarcely gets beyond showing what he feels and thinks about other painters past and present. In other words, he paints his comment and criticism instead of writing it.

Then he must not have the ambition to become a fashionable portraitist and to exhibit at the annual cattle show, at the Royal Academy. Effigies and icons of field-marshals, admirals, royalties, ladies of fashion, do not nowadays conduce to art ; for the uniforms, the decorations, the gowns, the coiffure in these strange anthropological exhibits are expected to absorb the painter's energy with little left over for the creation and interpretation of character. An effigy, the British public must learn, is a work of art only in the sense that Madame Tussaud's wax-works are works of art.

Having learnt to draw and then the relatively

easier discipline of painting, let the artist express himself—if he can afford to wait so long.

If not—there's the rub—how is one to provide for his livelihood without reducing him to be the slave of a sordid dealer or other kinds of task-masters ? In the States, after the panic of 1929, the New Deal tried to make work for thousands of painters at public expense. They were kept alive, but I have not heard of the masterpieces they have created.

Which leads me to a prime consideration, namely the need of turning public opinion against persons too lazy and incompetent for any kind of hard work being allowed to take to painting as an easy and economically and socially remunerative career, expecting to live on private sympathy and public doles the whole of their long lives. Indeed I have dreamt of societies for the suppression of unpromising painters. If despite discouragement they make good they will be much the better for it.

So much for the painters. And now for the propaganda. There is no lack of a certain sort. Indeed far too much, but it is apt to be cranky, cliquy, fanatically sectarian. It seldom takes hold of the people who count at home and almost never gets abroad.

Since the great period (1750–1840), no school of English painting has received the attention that the Pre-Raphaelites had, yet few of their canvases have left the country to go as missionaries for British art on the Continent and overseas. In our own day we have had in Augustus John a painter who, if, like Picasso, Soutine, Chagall, Dali, etc., etc., he had settled down in Paris, would now be selling like the most enriched of that glorious company. Being British, he was half-admired by the critics—how frightened they are when they try to speak seriously of a painter who is not Parisian!—taken up by society, became a dashingly smart Bohemian ; and the best of him is now engaged in writing his memoirs with a verve and brilliance he would have done better to devote to his art. I know of no other professional painter in our midst who could be marketed in the States and bring in much-needed dollars. There is to be sure a non-professional who, if he consented to exhibit his output in New York, Chicago and San Francisco and accompanied them with his presence, might bring back millions. I need not name him. Patriot though he is, he will scarcely submit to the role of *Boule de Suif*.

Finally the English must be more tactful as

well as more hospitable, caressing, flattering even to individuals of their own language group whether they come from New Zealand or New Brunswick, from the Cape or Colorado. Even if it cannot be done by generous hosts or state-endowed hostesses, there should always be on hand a Vollard or two to receive influential critics from abroad, with the sure hope that they will return to their homes praising and magnifying English studios and their output. Then and only then shall England be able to export articles that require little outlay for raw materials and relatively little labour and incidental expenses.

I Tatti
Settignano
December 1946

III

AN ILLUSTRATED CODEX OF THE MASTER OF SAN MINIATO

In the autumn of 1947 both Lord Crawford and Sir Kenneth Clark told me of illuminated pages in a manuscript that might be by Benozzo Gozzoli, recently discovered in the British Museum by the keeper of its Print Room, Mr. A. E. Popham. On request this gentleman, with the generous consent of his trustees, sent me photographs of some of the twenty-four illuminations. Thanks to so much kindness I can offer students reproductions of five of them and attempt to ascertain when they were done and by whom.

As Mr. Popham tells me, the illuminations of this manuscript (Harleian 1340) illustrate the prophecies of Joachim of Flora and " confirm to the pattern of the numerous illustrated manuscripts of the Prophecies ". I shall not deal with the symbolical or allegorical contents of

these little paintings, leaving that fascinating task
to competent philologers, particularly as I am
not sure it would add to our understanding of
their specific quality nor to our enjoyment of their
mysterious quaintness which so strongly appeals
to the child each of us still carries within himself.
I will approach them as a student of form and
style without discussing the colour which I have
not seen. We begin by describing them :

Pope John XVII (A.D. 1003) stands frontally
with keys held upright in his right hand and in
his left a palmette divided into seven curving bits
(is it not rather a kind of " flagellum " ?). A
sword reaches from his mouth to the shoulder of a
lamb, a lamb with a halo behind its head, and a
banner inscribed with a cross. To our right, a
winged monster (demon ?) with naked torso,
caterpillar body and serpent's tail, but wearing
a mitre, stretches his hands towards the lamb
which in turn looks at him. Above the pope's
keys a dove. (Plate 5.)

Pope Clement IV (A.D. 1265/1268) on horse-
back rides to our left. In middle distances a
wood behind rocks and nearer to the eye the
choir of a church. In its vestibule appears a
maiden with clasped hands. (Plate 6.)

Pope Martin IV (A.D. 1281/1285) is seen on a

paved platform like the last, but in profile to our
left.   He stoops to pierce a prostrate eagle with
a lance that ends not in a simple point but more
as a *fleur-de-lis*.   One may venture to suggest that
possibly the representation refers to the part this
pope took in favour of Charles d'Anjou against
the Hohenstaufen interests.   (Plate 7.)

Pope Honorius IV (A.D. 1285/1287), standing,
holds the keys in his right hand and lifts his left
as if surprised to see a slender youth wielding a
knotted club.   At the feet of the youth the head
of a young man.   (Plate 8.)

Pope Urban V (A.D. 1362/1370) sits frontally
against a Renaissance niche.   In his right a plant
(a " flagellum " ?) like the one held by Pope
John XVII, and in his left hand the keys.   At
his feet a peacock, while to right an angel touches
him on the shoulder and the hand of God pierc-
ing clouds blesses him.   (Plate 9.)

At first blush these miniature paintings recall
Benozzo and are, it is true, close to him and
scarcely unworthy of him.   Nor do we perceive
any element of costume or style or date to make
us hesitate in attributing them to him.   The last

E.A.—C

pope mentioned in this manuscript is Eugene IV, who died in 1447, when Gozzoli was in his twenty-seventh year and working in the style of these designs. The two youthful female heads, the one on the Clement and the other on the Urban sheet, are easy to match in the miniature altarpiece from the Cook Collection as well as in the *Rape of Helen*, both in the London National Gallery and both now unhesitatingly attributed to the young Benozzo. Also the folds of the draperies recall him.

Yet it is these folds that recall more closely another and inferior hand. They run more parallel, have deeper furrows and the loops tend to end more sharply than in Benozzo. Suspicion is aroused ; one notes that the profiles are harsher and the action less articulate, stiffer. Looking further and further we end by perceiving the hand of another artistic personality, one that was isolated and integrated and first published in 1913 under the name of the *Master of San Miniato* in my catalogue of Italian pictures in the J. G. Johnson Collection of Philadelphia. In 1936, in my *Italian Painters of the Renaissance*, I gave a list of the paintings then known to me by this little master. I have gone over this list again, comparing each entry with its photograph.

Surely no properly prepared student who had access to the same photographs would feel justified in excluding any, or at most one or two : the Pietà, for instance, reproduced p. 828 of Dedalo.[1]

These eclectic little masters tried to adopt the type and manners of the artists whose humble assistants they may have been, working now with one and now with the other, caricaturing and reducing manner to mannerism. Yet they had constants of their own, not lasting perhaps from the beginning to the end of their career, but long enough to connect one phase of it with the other. In our case, the folds of the draperies in the miniatures should be compared with such early works by our painter as the Lyons (Plate 10) and the former Auspitz Entombments, the Lazzaroni Madonna now in the Accademia di San Luca in Rome and the Saint Nicholas with Four Female Saints in the Courtauld Institute in London. Look, for instance, at the folds of the Mother of our Lord in the Lyons picture and at those of *Pope Martin IV* (Plate 7). On the other hand,

[1] A certain number of reproductions may be found in the *Burlington Magazine*, XLVI (1925), pp. 230 *et seq.*, in the *Bollettino d'Arte*, N.S., VI (1927), pp. 529 *et seq.*, and in Dedalo, XII (1933), pp. 819 *et seq.*, as well as in Van Marle, XVI, pp. 199–204.

the faces of the two old men in the Lyons picture link up with others that occur throughout his entire career.

In my *Italian Painters of the Renaissance* I described the San Miniato Master as active in the second half of the Quattrocento and as a follower of Fra Filippo and Botticelli. We now should infer that he began with the young Benozzo and toward 1447 had attained skill enough to paint our illuminations. We may add that he lived long enough to turn out works like the altarpiece in Kentucky, as soft and pleasant as Raffaellino del Garbo's. The leaflets here studied show him in an earlier phase than any known to us previously and also in subjects other than the usual Madonnas and Pietàs.

I have to confess that I perceive only now, guided by these illuminations, how much of Benozzo there is in the earlier works of our painter in his children particularly. Look, for instance, at the one reproduced by Van Marle in vol. XVI, p. 204.

In my *Drawings of Florentine Painters*, I ventured to suggest that a pen-sketch in the Malcolm

Collection of the British Museum (Ber. 906,
fig. 189) might be by Giusto d'Andrea instead of
Raffaellino del Garbo to whom it was attributed.
It represents (Plate 11) a rather youthful pope
with falcon on his wrist, riding out proudly while
in a doorway, to our right, a female with hands
crossed kneels in prayer. At the bottom of the
leaflet this hawking pope is labelled, in a hand
closely resembling Giusto d'Andrea's, as Clement
V and not IV. The resemblance between this
sketch and our Fig. 4 is close enough to make one
question whether they are not by the same craftsman, namely, the Master of the San Miniato
altarpiece. The inscription could not have been
put there by the artist himself, who would not
have made the mistake. It therefore invalidates
the suggestion that the handwriting must have
been by the author of the drawing. If the
inscription is by Giusto d'Andrea, then it must
have been jotted down when it came into his
possession.

Close as painting and pen-sketch are, there are
marked differences in the folds of the draperies.
They are less parallel, less pulled out, more
curving, more cursive. There is at the same time
so much more alertness, more pride in the horse-
man of the sketch. One is left wondering. It is

not rare to find a sketch more alive than the painting for which it served.

*   *   *

My conclusion is that the value of these illustrations to Joachim of Flora's prophecies consists not only in their revealing to us an earlier and hitherto unknown phase of the Master of San Miniato, but in their entertaining and unusual subject matter which gives us a welcome change from the endless Madonnas with or without Saints or the well-known scenes from the Gospels.

I Tatti
Settignano
January 1948

IV

ZANOBI MACHIAVELLI

Apart from the fun of the chase, there is little reason for wasting time over minor painters and sculptors. The only valid excuse is that they have clung so close to the great masters whom they imitated and served that hitherto they have been identified with them. While trying to scrape away the disfiguring barnacles and to restore the pure outline of an artistic personality, we may even get glimpses into the workshop of the great artists. That is why I venture to speak of so small a figure as Zanobi Machiavelli.

It is not intended here to recount the story of his career. That seems to have passed like the career of other minor masters, in aiding or imitating the great ones when these needed help, as probably was the lot of the San Miniato Master, the Castello Nativity Master, and even of the Carrand Triptych Master and of Alunno di Domenico.[1] If they lived long enough, they ended far from their beginnings. Thus the San Miniato Master began somewhere near Fra Angelico and ended as a rustic imitator of Botticelli, while the Castello Nativity Master started from Fra Angelico himself and lived to feel the influence of young Filippino Lippi (see, for instance, his Annunciation in San Giovanni dei Cavalieri, Florence). While aiding the creative artists and under their instruction, they could do charming things—as we see Zanobi did, although he ended as one of the crudest and most stereotyped of Quattrocento Florentines.

I must not miss the opportunity of saying that it is relatively easy to trace these painters through all phases. They give themselves away by a look, by an arabesque in the fold of their draperies

[1] Since these appellations were first made the actual names of the two last have been found. They are Giovanni di Francesco and Bartolommeo di Giovanni. I stick to the former appellations because Giovanni di Francesco and Bartolommeo di Giovanni tell me nothing, whereas Carrand Triptych Master and Alunno di Domenico tell me where they started from. It is like calling streets and roads and thoroughfares by the names of the places they lead to, as Avenue du Bois or Avenue du Trocadero, instead of what they now are called (for how long?), Avenue Président Wilson and Avenue Foch.

or by some other trick in the drawing of hands, hair, etc. Real connoisseurship is not concerned with artists who have such recognizable petty mannerisms, but with mighty geniuses like Titian or Velasquez and with talented imitators like Palma Giovane, like Padovanino, like Maffei, like Mazo.

To return to Machiavelli, he was at his best when working with or for his superiors and under their guidance and inspiration. He then could do something as attractive as the Madonna formerly in the Hurd Collection in New York (Plate 12).

At first glimpse it looks like a Filippo Lippi, to whom it is attributed. The sensitive, somewhat pouting youthful face reminds us of many painted by that artist between, say, 1440 and 1450 or so. Yet the crinkled, corkscrew bundled folds of the Virgin's kerchief are not his, nor the fingers of her left hand, nor the Child with its hair so delicately combed and meticulously parted in the middle. These are all characteristic of Zanobi Machiavelli, only not so coarse and mechanical as in his stereotyped mature phase under the influence of Benozzo Gozzoli.

In the same manner as the Hurd picture and close to Fra Filippo is a Madonna in a niche at

Sant' Andrea a Botinaccio, near Florence, which in 1936 in the Italian edition of my *Italian Pictures of the Renaissance* I listed as Fra Filippo (g.p.). Now it looks to me like a Machiavelli (Plate 13).

Later by two or three years but still under Fra Filippo's overpowering influence comes a Madonna that appeared at a sale (N/30) in the Parke-Bernet Galleries of New York on March 2, 1950 (Plate 14). The Child is obviously the same as in the Hurd picture. The Madonna's right hand closely foreshadows her right hand in the Besançon picture (Plate 20). The folds over her left hand resemble the ones in the Hurd *Madonna* (Plate 12). The head of the Madonna has a beauty, a graciousness, a look worthy of a real artist, which Machiavelli seldom was. Yet it is not quite Filippo's, although it comes near to such Madonnas as, for instance, the one from Berlin now in the National Gallery at Washington or the one in the Annunciation in the Palazzo Barberini at Rome (Pittaluga, pls. 44, 43).[1]

[1] Mary Pittaluga, *Filippo Lippi* (Del Turco Editore, Firenze, 1949). One of the few best monographs on a Quattrocento master that have appeared in years. It reproduces every painting that can be attributed to the artist and the Catalogue *raisonné* is a model of what it should be. I know no other so helpful. Almost it dis-

Let me call attention to a Madonna at Goettingen that seems to me by the Master of the Castello Nativity (Plate 15).[1] It surely must have been done after a similar sketch by Fra Filippo and in his workshop, probably at the same time that Machiavelli did the one we have just been studying (Plate 14).

Slightly earlier in date is a Madonna in the Galleria Carrara at Bergamo (Plate 16). It puzzled me for years and at one time I thought it might be by Domenico di Bartolo (then as now an absurd dump). Later I thought of the Carrand Master, and in the Italian edition of my *Pictures of the Italian Renaissance* I entered it with a question mark under Boccatis imitating Fra Filippo. Clearly it is by Machiavelli as the Child's hair and hands and the Madonna's hands lead us to conclude. It must have been done about 1437, the time that Lippi painted the Corneto Madonna and in quick succession the Louvre Madonna and Saints and the Bache

penses with a text : and I wonder whether in future serious and not fancy appreciation and interpretation had not better be included in the catalogue while texts could be abolished altogether.

[1] Until we learn just what has happened to works of art in Germany since the last war it surely will be less confusing to refer to them as in the museums where we knew them before 1939.

Madonna (Pittaluga, pls. 9, 12, 17). Most
probably painted in Lippi's studio and perhaps
a version of a lost work of that artist.

There can be little doubt that the four
Madonnas just discussed (Plates 12, 13, 14 and
16) are by Machiavelli. I am bold enough to
propose attributing to him two or three still
earlier works.

The first of the pictures I have in mind is a
little model for an altarpiece in the Musée Condé
at Chantilly (Plate 17 : Plate XI in Gruyer's
Catologue of 1896).[1] It represents the Virgin
enthroned between Peter and Anthony with six
angels between them. The types are Fra
Filippo's of about 1440, but the execution is so

[1] It is 20 by 16 centimetres in size, too small for even a
private chapel and most likely the *modello* for an altarpiece,
to be shown to the client who ordered the work (let us
hope that this may be discovered some day). By the way,
it would be desirable to make a study of these *modelli* and
of their relation more or less faithful to the completed
painting. As coming from Fra Filippo's studio, beside this
Chantilly one, I know of a " modello " in the Loeser
Collection at Florence, of another in the Collection of
Count Vittorlo Cini at Venice and of a third in the Fitzwilliam Museum at Cambridge. The last reproduced by
Pittaluga, pl. 205.

little his that I always have attributed it to Pesellino still in his master's studio. That attribution has been accepted by a number of serious students, yet it never quite satisfied me. If I left it in my various publications it was in the hope that my not hitting the mark would not misdirect others from doing it.

Now it looks as if it had better be ascribed to Machiavelli. The negroid curls of the angels and their draperies lead me to that conclusion, as do the wedge-like creases in the elbow of Saint Anthony, close to the ones in the Bergamo *Madonna* (Plate 16).

Earlier still may be the Tabernacle in the Walter's Art Gallery at Baltimore (Plate 18 : N/587 of old catalogue), obviously done before Machiavelli began to assist Fra Filippo. It represents in the central panel the Virgin enthroned between Francis and Sebastian while the Child gives the ring to Saint Catherine of Alexandria. The right wing has Tobias with the Archangel, Saint James and perhaps San Galgano ; while on the left one we find the *Magdalen*, Barbara, Apollonia and Lucy. Here again it is the folds that link it up with Machiavelli's Filippesque work.

The type and proportions are still of Fra

Angelico's followers, particularly of Giusto d'Andrea. To the same early phase belongs a delightful altarpiece, an Annunciation in my own parish church, San Martino a Mensola (Plate 19). I venture to ascribe it to Machiavelli as I find in it the same little folds as in all his paintings, whether early or late. The over-elaborate crumply curls of Gabriel are identical with those in the Chantilly picture (Plate 17).

To let the reader have a notion of what Machiavelli's later work was like, when he was left free to his own wooden self, I reproduce three characteristic paintings :

(1) A Madonna at Besançon (Plate 20 : Legs Gigoux N/263), where the Child as a whole, His hair and its Mother's hair, retain sufficient resemblance to what we find in the Hurd Madonna to justify the conclusion that they are by the same painter. Note the Virgin's right hand with its inarticulated fingers, as if made of wood or ivory.

(2) A Madonna with two Angels, formerly in the Aynard Collection at Lyons and

bequeathed by the late Mr. Maitland Griggs to the Yale University Museum (Plate 21). Again the Child, the hair, and this time the corkscrew folds justify the attribution of the Hurd picture to Machiavelli. So does the left hand of the Madonna, if compared with the right hand in the Hurd picture.

(3) An altarpiece that used to belong (as late as 1924) to Mr. Charles Livijn (Plate 22). Again the same Child, similar folds in draperies and all but identity between right hand of Saint James and left hand of Our Lady in Hurd Madonna.

In all of them we find the same traces of exaggeration that helped us to recognize Machiavelli in the paintings which we suppose done in Fra Filippo's studio : the crumply curls, the stiff, lifeless hands (imitations of hands in the Bache and other contemporary paintings by the master) the creased folds and draperies.

My conclusion is that an inferior artist can climb to unexpected heights in the studio of a great master, heights which his independent work could never have led us to suspect.

I recommend this subject as worthy of attention. Instead of manufacturing monographs full of unilluminative erudition and so exhaustive as to exhaust the reader, some of my young colleagues should devote themselves to the study of the inferior artist in the superior master's studio and of what shape he took when left to himself.

I Tatti
Settignano
November 1950

V

IMPORTANCE OF FASHION IN THE DATING OF PICTURES

Without the aid of a proper chronology the construction of an artistic personality is difficult. Unless a given picture can be inserted convincingly in a progressive series, I for one cannot admit it as a certain work by the master.

Let me cite an instance : I could not accept the altarpiece in the Rucellai Chapel at Santa Maria Novella as being by Duccio. I could not fit it into the series of his works as we used to date them. But when it became clear that it could be placed at the beginning of his career along with the great East window of 1285 in the cathedral of Siena I no longer hesitated to attribute it to him.

In the same way the late Aldo De Rinaldis, a conscientious student if ever there was one, would not accept the exquisite Beato Novello altarpiece in the church of Sant' Agostino in

E.A.—D

Siena as a work by Simone Martini (Plate 23).
I have no doubt that he would have changed his
mind if he could have realized, as we do now, that
it is earlier than any of the mature Simones
hitherto known.   It is the last link in a chain that
leads back to the Massa Marittima altarpiece,
attributed traditionally to Duccio and by recent
criticism to Segna.

I can recall with what despair I used to regard
the question of dating. My revered master,
Morelli, gave no clue for it. It occurred to me
finally that the dress of the figures, the furniture,
the frames even of pictures might help to date
them.

To confine ourselves here to dress alone, the
problem has its own complications. These arise
from the fact that fashions in former days took
time to travel from place to place, more time in
the centuries when communications were difficult
than in more recent ones, and naturally lasted
much longer where they had penetrated with
difficulty.

From the XIIIth century on, Paris was, with
rare interruptions, the centre from which fashions
spread in every direction. Early in the XVth
century Milan seems to have furnished style in
dress to the rest of Italy. Towards the middle

of the same century the Burgundian court began to exercise an all-pervading influence, particularly on Ferrara. The two feudal courts seem to have been in such close touch that what was worn in the first soon reappeared in the second. From Ferrara it spread quickly to the aristocrats of Bologna, more slowly to the plutocrats of Florence, and eventually to the courtesans of Rome.

The student therefore cannot be too cautious in allowing for the time-lag in the introduction of fashions to the different parts of a country. The dress that would be worn at Ferrara and Bologna, Venice and Milan might not appear in Florence till five years later and in Umbria five or ten years later still.

On the other hand, in connection with the exhibition now (1951) being prepared in Turin, it may be found useful to catalogue costume from the study of frescoes and panel pictures that we know to have been done at a definite place. Thus the admirable and detailed representation of dress in Carlo Crivelli's paintings (Plate 24) offer a repertoire of fashion of the second half of the XVth century as worn in the Marches of Ancona which, being so accessible by sea from Venice, did not lag too far behind the northern centres of taste. On the contrary, the costumes shown in the frescoes by Andrea Delicio at Atri in the Abruzzo, or those of Saturnino Gatti at Tornimparte near Aquila, are decades behind those worn at that date in northern cities (Plate 26). In as remote a place as Cascia the frescoes in the old chapel of Santa Rita represent people whose dress is generations behind what was being worn at Ferrara and Milan at that date.

I can allow myself but one example to illustrate what I have been trying to suggest.

In the National Gallery of Ireland there is a predella representing the Adoration of the Magi (Plate 25). I reproduce the left side of it only, where behind the three kings a kneeling page offers a crown. It seems that the attractiveness of the treatment has recalled Giorgione and that some students would like to attribute it to his close following.

In a sense, the entire Venetian Cinquecento keeps reminding one of Giorgione. But specifically this predella seems close to the young Tintoretto, that is to say, thirty years after Giorgione's death. This may of course be regarded as a mere guess on my part, but what is indisputable is that the puff on the hip of the kneeling page was not worn before 1540 or so. That clinches the matter. Such a detail of costume would not appear in the immediate following of Giorgione.

These few words could be enlarged into a book, but I trust will suffice to point the way to what help art historians can find in the study of costume.

I Tatti
Settignano
March 1951

VI

A "SACRA CONVERSAZIONE" IN
THE LOUVRE

From the moment that in the Louvre sixty-four years ago I first laid eyes on the picture I am going to discuss now, it fascinated me by its glowing warmth, its saturated colouring, its statuesque personages so contented with mere existence, so silently happy to be together (Plate 27). The fact that it was then attributed to Giorgione helped to attach me to this canvas. To-day it may not be easy to realize what it meant to a young American with Walter Pater's siren music singing in his heart to see this magic name " Giorgione " under a picture. It was sheer ecstasy.

Two or three years in Italy increased my worship of the artist, but began to make me question whether all the pictures labelled in galleries, or considered to be by him in churches, were his handiwork. Of the two attributed to him in the Louvre, the subject of this article no longer seemed to be by him. I began to speculate about its authorship.

The Bergamasque Cariani was then coming to the fore as the possible author of doubtfully attributed Giorgionesque paintings, and I was not alone perhaps in assigning to him the Louvre picture and a far greater one, the Glasgow *Christ and the Adulteress*.[1] Surely Cariani was not altogether unworthy of attention, as is proved by the composition in the Bergamo Gallery of a woman playing the lute, while by her sits a nude asleep—a subject and treatment that has everything of Giorgione, except his quality of mind and hand (Plate 28). At his best, Cariani is too flimsy, too sketchy and, except for one or two paintings like the one just mentioned, too provincial to have painted anything so studied, so robust, so impressive, as this Louvre masterpiece.

But if neither Giorgione nor Cariani painted it, to whom shall we turn? It now bears the label of Sebastiano del Piombo. For twenty years or more, in fact ever since Lionello Venturi rediscovered Domenico Mancini, I have been tempted more and more to attribute it to him.

[1] After seeing this picture again at the Giorgione exhibition in Venice (1955) I no longer doubt that it is by the great master himself.

Let us now look at our picture (Plate 27 : Louvre n° 1135) in the light of all that I have learned since I first saw it more than sixty years ago.

It is an oblong composition, not unlike such early Titians as the Madrid Madonna with SS. Ulfius and Bridget, the Louvre Madonna with SS. Ambrose and Maurice, the Vienna Madonna with the cherries, the Dresden Madonna with four saints.[1] Here the Madonna sits in all but complete profile to our right, holding on her knees the Child, who looks benignly on a donor, whose bust only is seen, facing to our left. On our right appears Saint Sebastian. Between him and the Madonna a young female saint,[2] with her right hand to her breast, faces the Child as if contemplating Him. To the extreme left, the bust of an elderly, bald, bearded Saint Joseph, again in profile to our right. Behind the Virgin a curtain. Over and between the others a landscape with romantic distances. Saint Sebastian stands under an oak, the leaves of which are stencilled against the sky.

[1] All too easily accessible nowadays in various picture books on Titian to require reproduction here.

[2] In a contemporary copy to be mentioned later she holds an arrow for Saint Ursula.

I will not attempt to describe the colour in detail. I recall cherry-reds and yellows and greens more Titianesque than Titian, the reds particularly.

Delightful is the movement of the Child, held in around the baby waist by the tip end of His mother's kerchief, as He leans forward on her knee, and beautiful is the way her hand embraces His knee.

The head of the donor is a typical Giorgion-esque portrait of the second decade of the XVIth century.

So close to Titian is this painting that I must give the reasons why I do not believe it to be by him. There are faults he would not have committed. I will enumerate some of them. There is a disproportion in the size of the heads. The torso of Saint Sebastian reminds one too much of a fleshy Antinous, as Titian's in the Salute altarpiece does not. His mouth is open as if to scream with pain (Plate 32), but the expression of the face is not of suffering. The lower hand of the female Saint is badly drawn. The folds of the draperies are too heavy, as if quilted instead of being unlined or thinly lined textiles. Then there are the leaves on the oak-tree. They are too leathery. Finally, the tonality of the whole is too rich, too fiery.

A further reason for not assigning this work to Titian himself is that the female Saint and the Saint Joseph are both too archaic in type and still too Bellinesque for Titian, in the phase that inspired the author of the Louvre picture, whoever he was.

The phase of Titian's artistic personality that I refer to is represented by works mentioned already and by others like the portrait supposedly of Caterina Cornaro from the Crespi and Cook Collections and now in the National Gallery of London, but best of all by the frescoes in the Scuola del Santo at Padua (Plate 29). Our painter not only echoes, so to speak, shapes, forms and action of these compositions, but the colouring as well. In these Santo frescoes the technique preludes the gradations, nuances and blending feasible with tempera and oil glazes, and Titian's colouring appears in them less fused, less harmonized, less toned than on panel and canvas.

"Whoever he was," I said just now of the author of the Louvre picture. Who he was, is not easy to say.

Let me open a parenthesis.

The attribution of works of art is seldom a matter of exact science, and in many cases one cannot rely on the superposition of a part of an unclassified picture on an ascertained one and conclude that the two coincide. They may coincide, and yet the quality as the spirit may be different. Both quality and spirit escape exact measurement and therefore remain, as the Germans call it, " highly subjective ".

Because the attribution of all but stereotyped works remains so " subjective ", it partakes of the nature of art rather than of science. It is a matter of intuition, of inspiration even, like all creative arts, and not of demonstration. Indeed, it may be taken on a humbler level and compared with the art of the wine- and tea-taster.

I cannot demonstrate that the picture before us was painted by Domenico Mancini, but I can plead for it.

First and foremost, by excluding other attributions.

Nobody in this late day will want to ascribe the picture to Giorgione, and I trust I have succeeded in giving reasons why it is not by Titian, although so close to him. None of the other immediate followers of Giorgione, except one presently to be mentioned, is likely to be

accepted as the painter of this same picture.
Surely neither Palma Vecchio, nor Luzi of
Feltre, nor Boselli of Bergamo, nor the younger
Girolamo da Treviso, nor the author of the Pitti
Tree Ages (that used to be given to Lotto). In
recent years a serious attempt has been made
to ascribe it to Sebastiano del Piombo. Its chief
defender has been Professor Pallucchini.[1]

Sebastiano del Piombo is an artist who has
occupied me for sixty years, because he belongs
at once to the Venetian and to the Florentine
schools, the two that have been the chief subjects
of my studies. I feel as if I knew him, as I know
my most intimate life-long friends. I know that
in his Venetian phase and in the earliest Roman
one, he is very close to Giorgione and captures
no little of his elegance of line, charm of colour
and magic of light and shade. In these same
years he is never so bulky, so rough even, as is the
author of the Louvre picture. His shapes may
be ample, as in his Adoration of the Shepherds in
the Fitzwilliam Museum of Cambridge, or in the
Death of Adonis in the Uffizi : to my eye and
feeling they are emptier and lighter. And
Sebastiano, except in what both he and Titian
take from Giorgione, never recalls Titian nor

[1] R. Pallucchini, *Sebastian Viniziano* (Mondadori, 1944).

does he ever imitate him. Our painter on the other hand is, as we have seen, so close to Titian in every way, that he may have seen and remembered the latter's Saint Sebastian of the Salute and even copied out and out some Madonna now lost. In a word, he is less linear and more pictural than Sebastiano.

I feel almost as certain that our picture was painted by the individual who signed the Madonna with the Music-making Angel at Lendinara (Plate 30); or rather I feel certain enough to propose the attribution as putting us on the road that may lead us to the author of this work.

The proof I have to offer is in demonstrable terms light. Indeed, it consists no more than in the strong resemblance between the head of the angel in the Lendinara altarpiece (Plate 31), and the head of the Saint Sebastian in the Louvre picture (Plate 32). If you allow for a considerable advance towards a more pictural style in the last, and if you make both the heads face the same way, the likeness in features, in treatment of the hair, in the drawing and modelling of nose and mouth, and then in pose and even in expression—the likeness is, I say, great enough to make it probable that they are by the same hand.

Again and again, hundreds of times again, I have found a clue to an attribution in a point of resemblance as slight as this, and far more often than not it has turned out to be the right one. The resemblance between the two heads is even more striking in the shadowgraph (X-ray) : the stumpy short nose with the uncertain drawing of nostrils, the flabby mouth and fleshy lips.

Unfortunately we have no other signed or documented work by Domenico Mancini, nor do we know how long he lived.[1] In the Lendinara picture he signs himself as a Venetian, and in fact his Madonna there is almost copied from the one in Giovanni Bellini's altarpiece of 1506 at San Zaccaria. His later career remains a matter of inference. If I am right in ascribing the Louvre picture to him, then he must have lived on a few years more, and been still young enough to make rapid progress.

Thus we see him in a portrait in the Borghese Gallery dated 1510 (Plate 33). It has the same colouring, almost identical modelling and mouth

[1] Fullest account of him with reproductions, in Johannes Wilde, " Die Probleme um Domenico Mancini " in *Jahrbuch der Kunsthistorischen Sammlungen in Wien*, 1933, pp. 113–18 and 129–31. See also Carlo Gamba, " Contributo alla conoscenza di Domenico Mancini " in *Critica d'Arte*, XXIX, 1949, pp. 211–17.

(though closed) and nostrils as in the angel of the Lendinara picture, but as yet no touch of the Giorgionesque lyricism of that figure. It could almost be taken for a work by the meticulous but rather dull Bergamasque follower of Giovanni Bellini, Andrea Previtali.

The *Two Lovers* that used to be at Dresden and in the Scarpa Collection at Motta di Livenza, do not concern us here. The originals are for the most part either inaccessible or not to be traced, and adequate reproductions are not to be had. Happily they would throw no light on the present task, which is to assign the Louvre picture to Domenico Mancini.

Many years ago I saw a nearly contemporary copy of this work by a tenth-rate painter whose hand I have recognized elsewhere (Plate 34). It was made for a donor who wanted his portrait inserted instead of the one in the original, a fairly common procedure with Bellinesque pictures.

Without any deep conviction that it is by Domenico Mancini, I venture to add to this group another painting that to my knowledge has hitherto escaped attention.

It is a canvas measuring $1 \cdot 02 \times 0 \cdot 74$ metres, that once upon a time belonged to a Herr Mallmann who resided at Blaschkow in Germany

(Plate 35). It represents an opulent lady in gorgeous dress and tiara both studded with huge pearls and precious stones. She points to a head held over a tub by a swarthy, shaggy young man. The tub is decorated with a winged lion's head, painted in a way that reminds one of the winged coat of arms in the Dresden *Two Lovers*.

What is visible of the landscape reminds us of the one of the *Two Lovers* formerly in the Scarpa Collection at Motta di Livenza (Plate 36). More to our purpose is the fact that the hand of Thomiris—for it is she—pointing at the head of Cyrus is so very much like the hand of the female saint in our picture. The features of the same Thomiris could be a development of the Virgin there and the young man of the Saint Sebastian. But these are mere fancies.

When I saw this picture many many years ago, the owner assured me that the lady bore the features of Caterina Cornaro. Not impossible, and the winged lion of Saint Mark's on the tub would seem to point to some allegory. I recommend its interpretation to the iconographers who now crowd the ranks of art historians.

In the two last editions of my *Italian Pictures of the Renaissance* (Oxford, 1932, and Milan, Hoepli, 1936) I have given a small and partly tentative list of the pictures I would attribute to Domenico Mancini. To these I could now only add two, namely Count Gamba's *Madonna with Two Saints* (Plate 37), which I saw for the first time in his house in 1946, and a *Christ and the Adulteress* (Plate 38) attributed to Giorgione which during my last visit to the Musée Condé at Chantilly, reminded me more of Mancini than of anybody else.

I Tatti
Settignano
April 1951

VII

GIOVAN BATTISTA TIEPOLO

This is not to be a variant on the kind of article that one may read in any serious encyclopedia, the Treccani or the equally praiseworthy Garzanti on Italian masters. At the age of 86, unless one is dealing with the exact sciences or with minute erudition, everything one writes tends to be autobiographical. So I shall speak of Tiepolo not with a pretence to what German scholars would call " objectivity " but as for sixty years off and on I have lived with him and thought and felt about him.

It should be remembered that outside of Venice Tiepolo was scarcely known or discussed in Italy and even less abroad. I vaguely recall that he first reached me more than sixty years ago through the then already famous American artist, John S. Sargent. Probably Sargent had been visiting his friends, Mr. and Mrs. Daniel Curtis, at the Palazzo Barbaro, Venice, and had discovered Tiepolo then and there. I know that he kept praising him to other painters and to all who would listen.

We nowadays may find it hard to believe that sixty-five years ago not only Tiepolo was unknown to the cultivated public but that even Velasquez was little more than a name and Greco still in the womb of oblivion. And it may be doubted whether the same public as yet had become familiar with the names of Cézanne and Degas.

Since then, how much has been written about these three old masters! As for Tiepolo, the writer to whom, far more than to any other, he owes his fame was Pompeo Molmenti. Indeed, his great monograph on that artist published in 1910 still remains the most classical and most comprehensive work on the subject. It tells everything worth knowing, and I now agree with most of his appreciation and estimates, as perhaps I should not have in my earlier years. I myself in my little book on the Venetian painters that appeared in 1894—sixteen years before Molmenti's work—spoke of Tiepolo in all but the highest terms as a craftsman but made certain reserves and expressed regret that as an illustrator he put before us a world so strutting, so haughty, so pompous.

I have changed my mind, owing to a maturer judgment and to a much wider and more penetrating acquaintance with his works. Ever and ever so many canvases have come to light in the last sixty years and they as a rule were more genial, more lyrical, more familiar and even more tender than his mural paintings. Many of them are still in the limbo of the market and others in private hands. I have seen all but few of them and can refresh memory with photographs. When one is thoroughly at home with an artist, owing to an assiduous acquaintance with his works, reproductions are as helpful as they are misleading to those who begin with them.

After all this tuning of instruments I can start telling what I now feel and think about Tiepolo as a craftsman and as an artist.

In the first place, as a master of the painter's craft.

In his earliest work his drawing frequently has a bite that might have become as bitter as Toulouse-Lautrec's. With time it grew gentler, more smoothed out and rhythmic. Like his Venetian predecessors, he did not put draughtmanship above and beyond all other qualities of visual representation. No doubt a Vasari of his day would have shaken his wig and sighed,

muttering as the great Florentine art historian
did over Titian, that really he might have been a
considerable artist if only he knew how to draw.

He was sufficient master of the nude to do what
he liked with it. An obedient instrument in his
vocabulary of representation, he never let himself
be tempted to show off what tricks he could
play with it, what acrobatic displays of skill,
although so much of his work, his ceiling frescoes
for instance (Plate 39), gave ample occasion for
both.

I will say nothing about his technique in the
narrowest sense of the word, for that is studio
talk which painters only can follow or profit by.
It is no more our concern as art lovers than the
cooking of the meal that we consume. Suffice
it to add that it is a technique which has resisted
time. Tiepolo's canvases and frescoes have
darkened and altered surprisingly little.

This leads me to his colour. In his early
works it tends to the bituminous and is contrasted
in a savoury way with brighter and even harsher
tints. Then, before reaching full maturity, his
tonality was already gay as his subjects required
and never foul or morose, not even where the
theme would have tolerated it. His biscuit
browns, his blues, his reds, his greys, his whites,

invariably transparent and radiant, are a joy to the eye and to the mind behind the eye.

At the same time he was a scene-setter of the most decorative kind. On all occasions and on all surfaces, his compositions never fail to make the utmost use of the space at his disposal. His grouping of personages, even of the most complicated crowds, is not only legible at sight but balanced in a way that is restfully harmonious.

Then his treatment of void space is most unusual. In his many ceiling compositions he succeeds in making one feel the utter remoteness of the sky, no matter how many the figures that seem to fill it (Plate 40).

These gifts and skills of the craftsman Tiepolo, the artist employed to introduce us to a world as healthy, as even-tempered and kindly and elegant as gay, as courteous, as festive, as amusing as any we have had since the Venetians of the XVIth century. He was at the same time a psychologist as few other painters ever have been. I know nobody who better than he could give the exact expression to face and body that his subject needed. No over-statement and no under-statement, any more than in Racine. Not even in scenes of martyrdom (Plate 41) or of the sacrifice of tender and lovely creatures like Iphigeneia

(Plate 42) or the daughter of Jeftha does he stir us to wild pity. Perhaps still more remarkable is his freedom from sentimentality in representations of the Holy Family (Plate 43) and of that ticklish subject *Saint Joseph with the Christchild*. In one of his flights into Egypt the Virgin fondles her Child as an angel with outspread wings rows the Holy Family over the Nile (Plate 44). I know nothing in biblical illustration more charming. (Reproduced as Plate 132 in Morassi's *Tiepolo*, Arti Grafiche, Bergamo, the best work on the subject since Molmenti.) The image he gives of the Saviour is the least unsatisfactory known to me. Not that that is saying much, for no human hand can depict what we would imagine Him to have looked like.

Tiepolo was likewise successful in representing fervour and ecstasy, as for instance in his Saint James of Compostella and in his Saint Tecla ad Este.

He was unsurpassed in court ceremonies and scenes of splendour and magnificence, as in his meeting of Anthony and Cleopatra, and other receptions in sumptuously palatial surroundings (Plate 45). Again in his mythological and romantic compositions, his Amphitrites, his Nereids, his Bacchanals, or in his subjects taken

from Tasso and Ariosto (Plates 46, 47). No
illustrator gayer, more radiant, more lyrical. His
landscape accompaniments with their tufted
groves, noble masonry, charming foregrounds
and nostalgic distances of sea and sky, have a
rival in Fragonard only. Indeed, Tiepolo can
compete with the best that the French masters
of the XVIIIth century could do, with Fragonard
and Boucher and Hubert Robert. He reminds
me of all three. His range is however much
wider than theirs. He paints or etches every
phase of life from the humblest to the sublimest
while they are more confined to subjects that
fringe on the erotic. It is by the way worthy of
note that unlike their French contemporaries, the
Italian masters of the XVIIIth century never paint
woman as an object of mere desire. Certainly
not Tiepolo.

For the psychologist and painter that Tiepolo
was, he seems to have done very few portraits.
Perhaps he was too busy. I know several drawings and sketches of heads, but only three so-
called portraits, and only one of note : the
Procurator Querini in his official robes. For
grasp of character and for execution it is unsurpassed in Italy after Tintoretto.

So he filled churches, palaces and villas from

Udine to Milan, from Bergamo to Venice, in Wuerzburg and Madrid. In the Royal Palace of Madrid and in the Residence of the Prince Bishop at Wuerzburg, he executed his most ambitious work as a fresco decorator. Among surviving schemes of painted narrative, allegory, idyll, there surely is none to compare with what he achieved. Achieved with an ease and more than ease, a joy in creation and a delight in execution which are communicated to the spectator and make Tiepolo's mural paintings among the most life-enhancing achievements of visual art. Why not the very highest? Perhaps there is in him an inclination to facility, although he never lowers himself to displays of dexterity. If we compare him with Paolo Veronese, whom he took for his model, he is more spirited, swifter, more sparkling, more nervous in touch, but less arresting, less convincing. He has less tactile values than a Veronese, a Titian, a Velasquez and even a Rubens—to speak only of his predecessors.

I have mentioned Veronese as the artist he aimed to equal. I have not yet spoken of his origins nor of the influence upon him of older contemporaries. Those matters no longer interest me. I am concerned with what an artist comes to, more than in the question of how he

got there and from where he started. It is
obvious that Tiepolo, to begin with, owed a great
deal to Sebastiano Ricci and something to
Piazzetta and even to Solimena and perhaps to
Magnasco. So no doubt did many other painters
who came to nothing.

It is amusing and illuminating to ask what
would have become of certain artists, say visual
artists, living at other times and other places
than those they actually lived in. What for
instance would Raphael have become, had he
been born in 1883 instead of 1483 and in Barcelona or Valencia instead of Urbino ? Would
he have ended as a Picasso, the Pablo Picasso
whose initial gifts as a draughtsman were so
much like his own ? And Michelangelo, can
you place him in the XVIIIth century and in
Paris instead of Rome ? And if he were living
now ? In which exhibition of the New York
Museum of Modern Art or the itinerant Peggy
Guggenheim Collection would he be rein-
carnated ? A hundred years ago there began
to flourish in England a sculptor and painter
who tried to be a Michelangelo and did not
altogether fail. But how many of those who
admire his Wellington monument in Saint Paul's
recall the name of Alfred Stevens !

To come back to Tiepolo. I can see him as a mural decorator at Alexandria, or Pergamon, or Antioch. Then I can see him again in the XVIth century as Paolo Veronese in all this artist's splendour. But I find it difficult to see him later and even in XVIIIth-century France, whose painters were so close to him and in their restricted way a touch more serious as craftsmen. And I cannot imagine him living in the last hundred years of ours. He surely would not have sunk to be a Besnard or a Zorn or even a Sargent. Only two artists flowering towards the end of the last century seem to have had gifts that might have rivalled his, had he been their contemporary. Living when they did, there was little scope for their talent. The greater artist of the two was Toulouse-Lautrec, of whose biting contours the young Tiepolo reminded us. The other was Cheret. The first confined himself to cynical portrayal of dissipated life. We admire his draughtsmanship while we vomit over his subject matter.

As for Cheret, his posters with the wit and verve and sparkle which we so enjoyed sixty years ago, were all that a Tiepolo then painting could have done. What else ? Where the churches, then or since, that would have ordered his altarpieces, where the royal palaces and patrician villas that would have wanted his frescoes, where the public festivals, the processions, the regattas, in dazzling costumes, Oriental as well as European, that an XVIIIth-century Venice commanded its painters to reproduce, where the fine livers that would have commissioned him to paint his mythological, allegorical and comic scenes, his *capricci*, where the patrons ready to buy his canvases as they came fresh from his brush ?

I end with reaffirming my deep conviction that although we cannot place Tiepolo alongside the very few greatest artists of all time, he yet was the greatest painter Italy has had since Tintoretto. None of the gods and idols so admired in our own day, not Magnasco, not Strozzi, not even Caravaggio, can be compared with him. I prophesy that he will be enjoyed when the others will have become subjects of mere erudition.

I Tatti
Settignano
May 1951

VIII

THE RESTORATION OF LEONARDO'S "LAST SUPPER"

Few problems are more controversial than the problem of how to restore a painting. I have never encountered a practitioner of that craft who approved of the work of another, and as for the layman, he is apt to take sides all the more violently the less he understands what it is all about. It can even become a matter for national prestige. For instance, the recent restorations of pictures in the London National Gallery are passionately defended by most English people against the almost universal disapproval of continental craftsmen and critics.

One of the reasons for this state of things is that there is no agreement about what there is to be done with an old painting that needs treatment. The French seem to hold that it is enough to clean a panel or canvas, to stop up holes revealed by the process and to leave it at that. Germans or German-trained believe that they can bring the picture back to the state it was in when it left the painter's hands.

A painting, no matter how well preserved, has undergone in the course of centuries all sorts of interior changes owing to the organic elements that not only deteriorate with time but are at war with each other. The hygrometric and thermometric conditions to which they have been exposed must also be taken into account.

Let me consider an example. Domenico Veneziano painted an altarpiece which is now in the Uffizi, while of three small panels originally forming its predella two are now in the National Gallery of Washington and one in the Fitzwilliam Museum of Cambridge, England. All these panels, big and little, were done at the same time, in the same studio and with the same technical procedure. No two of them look alike now in colour and tone.

The technique of the German schools was ever so much more robust than the one used by Italian painters. A German restorer can work away at a panel of his old masters as if it were oilcloth or marble or even metal. Indeed, many German old pictures look as burnished as copper pots and pans. Woe to the Italian work treated in the same way. I recall a Titian portrait done with delicate glazes that simply disappeared, leaving nothing but the underpainting, when treated by a famous Nordic restorer. An Italian painting should never be put at the mercy of any craftsman not Italian, or at least trained in Italy.

Restoration is not an affair of so-called scientific aids. X-rays, violet rays and all the complicated expensive machinery of the laboratories now installed in all the great public galleries can achieve little unless there is a gifted and experienced eye to direct them. The important part is the cleaning and it can be done only by one who knows what to expect. That demands in the first place an exact attribution, then the knowledge of the precise period in the painter's career in which the work to be restored was done. The practitioner thus prepared will know what to look for as he proceeds. Otherwise no spirits, no oils, no emulsions, "neither poppy nor mandragora nor all the oozy spices of the East" will help him to be a trustworthy restorer.

If he has the gift and experience and knowledge, a penknife, a razor, a drop of turpentine will suffice, as indeed I saw with my own eyes when the other day I witnessed what Professor

Pelliccioli was doing with Leonardo's famous *Last Supper* (Plates 48, 50).

I had heard that he was at work on it and went to Milan on purpose to meet him there. He allowed me to climb up to the platform on a level with the fresco, and as this platform was on wheels it could be pushed forward and backward. In that way I could look as close as if I were reading at what Professor Pelliccioli had already done, at what he was doing, and could let him explain to me what he still had to do (Plate 49).

The cleaned surface of the fresco, looked at with magnifying-glasses and under strong artificial light, appeared like a mosaic composed of tiny tesseræ of coloured glass. I felt I was touching bottom, that the multiple restorations of centuries had been removed and that I was looking at what Leonardo had painted, deteriorated by the centuries but no longer deturpated by incompetent hands.

Drawing back a few feet the mosaic effect disappeared and the figures came looming out of a haze, grand, massive, space-absorbing. They make one realize that Leonardo was more the precursor of the Cinquecento in the proportioning of the human figure and its relation to the given space than his exact contemporary Signorelli and more even than his younger rival Michelangelo.

When Professor Pelliccioli with his high competence has achieved this noble task, Leonardo's most famous creation will be visible as it has not been for generations. How one wishes a new Goethe could appear to write about it, as that genius did 180 years ago, now that one can see the composition relatively near to what Leonardo must have meant it to look like.

I seemed to discover, for instance, that the apostles did not, as in previous treatments of the *Last Supper*, sit one alongside the other but three behind three to each side of the Saviour. The play of hands, more expressive than elsewhere in the entire range of visual art, the beauty of a face like that of the apostle Philip, the atmosphere of the tragic moment are now coming to their own.

When I climbed down from the platform and from the floor looked up at the fresco I was amazed to find how little in ordinary daylight it carried. I would suggest either that the windows be greatly enlarged or that perhaps an arrangement of strong lamps could be thought out that would light the fresco up to its full value.

Rome
November 1953

E.A.—F

IX

PICASSO

For seventy years I have been looking at works of art of the last seventy centuries. They have shaped my aspirations, they have taught me to feel the charm of everyday things, they have revealed aspects of landscape that I never should have been seen left to myself, they have enlarged my horizon and have led me to enjoy not only animals but human beings as works of art. The well-proportioned, well-articulated man and woman, the shape of an arm, of a hand, of a wrist, of a leg, of an ankle, can give me the same pleasure that I derive from sculpture. In short, I have learnt to be, as it were, my own artist. And not that alone : the mere animal that I was at birth has been humanized through art.

With such experience, conditioning and consequent expectations I approach every object of visual art that I am privileged to see. This time it is the exhibition of Picasso's work held just now in Milan. It contains no end of pictures, some bits of sculpture, some ceramics and a number of engravings and book illustrations.

As Picasso's fame is based chiefly on his paintings, let us look at them first, before exhibition and gallery fatigue overpowers us.

His children, playing, riding, attitudinizing, comfortable, happy, strutting with animal *joie de vivre*, are captivating (Plate 51). A whiff of Marie Laurencin is exhaled by them and they are none the worse for it (Plate 52). The portrait head of his own mother is a deeply touching presentation of a woman who has loved and suffered and attained peace through resignation (Plate 53). The notation of this masterpiece betrays the artist's acquaintance with Van Gogh. With all these paintings in the first room I feel at home and happy.

Then come some massive ponderous *Mothers* modelled in the manner that a Peruvian ceramist might have used. They do not seem to be done directly from life (Plate 54).

What can I say of the other paintings? The world they belong to is not the world of art I have lived in. I am not acquainted, nor do I want to be acquainted, with its inhabitants.

Most of these paintings represent neither

human beings nor animals nor even monsters, but something resembling lay figures (*manne-quins*), geometrized, with many facets, eyes and eyes and again eyes, noses upon noses, noses over-lapping and getting more and more difficult to define, to recognize, let alone to understand (Plates 55, 56).

In others the human figure is reduced to an arabesque with buttocks—the *derrière béni* of the Thousand and One Nights tales—as most pro-minent feature, the neck serpentine, the head diminished to the shape, size and value of a stopper for a bottle.

As if tired of maltreating and misshaping the human body—far more so than Joyce was of using the words of his mother tongue—Picasso presents us with a series of canvases smeared over with criss-cross arrows that dart about like crazed and buzzing flies and have nothing in common with what we hitherto have regarded as painting. And except for the exterior fact of being done with pigments they cannot be called paintings. Nor do the epic compositions like the one called *Guernica* impress me as more than crude and vehement evocations of Greek Vase painting dashed with reminiscences of XIVth- and XVth-century frescoes representing the

Triumph of Death, like the Catalan one in the Picture Gallery of Palermo or Traini's in the Campo Santo of Pisa.

If that was all I had to say about Pablo Picasso I should have refrained from writing these few paragraphs. Merely negative criticism may amuse the performer and his public but is in no way constructive and certainly not interpretative. I have also much to say in his favour.

Picasso is what Vasari called the Renaissance artists, a master of " l'arte del Disegno ", and except in architecture he has tried his hand with signal success as engraver, as sculptor and, best of all, as ceramist. In all of these activities he manifests talents for draughtsmanship that have seldom been surpassed and along traditional lines. The other day, not in this exhibition, I saw one of his recent drawings of a woman's head that neither an Ingres nor even a Raphael would have disowned. Indeed, I recollect that when he was still utterly unknown to fame I was comparing him to Raphael.

In this exhibition his draughtsmanship is revealed in his sculptures, in his book illustration, in his engravings and above all in his ceramics. Indeed, I am led to ask myself whether when he turned away from traditional painting he had been aware of his gifts as a ceramist ? Would he not have been tempted to give up painting altogether for ceramics ?

In bronze or in ceramics his owls and fowls and indeed all his other animals, as we see in his illustrations to Buffon's *Natural History*, are comfortable, warm in themselves, happy in their perfect animality (Plates 57, 58).

At this point I want to draw attention to the fact that a creative artist can produce the same effects, whatever his medium may be, and is not the slave to material means as was taught for generations and is still accepted. It was certainly not for technical reasons that Picasso turned away from picture-making.

Being what I am, a lover of all the arts of the last seven thousand years, I naturally enjoy Picasso most when he is traditional. I delight in his classical moments when, like the great illustrator Flaxman or even the Icelandic Thorwaldsen, he returns to the pure Greek mode. We find him so on the plates representing a Duel of Centaurs or a Woman looking into a Mirror (Plates 59, 60) or in the huge lekythe with Dancing Menads or in the illustrations to Balzac's *Chef-d'œuvre Inconnu* or to Gongora's sonnets. I have seen Picasso's engraved portrait of this epoch-making Spanish baroque poet (not in this exhibition) that almost has the quality of a Velasquez.

I have given as sincere an appreciation of Picasso as my inveterate habits of valuing works of art will permit. I cannot touch here on what may be designated his psychology nor on the psychology of the worshippers and theologians of his paintings who with their metaphysical Gnostic or Freudian interpretation turn him into a cult hero of a new mysticism.

Rome
November 1953

X

ILLUMINATED MANUSCRIPTS

Illuminated manuscripts are not easily accessible to the public, and for good reasons. Most of them are still in codices and can be shown only two pages at the time. There is no other way unless the leaves are extracted and exhibited separately. This is not to be recommended as it takes away from their character as book illustration and besides makes them liable to lose or change colour or to fade away from permanent exposure to the light. Many of them are too fragile, indeed so fragile that most keepers of illuminated manuscripts would prefer to keep them like houris in a harem. Consequently the difficulties for the art lover of my type who just wants to enjoy these pages for their sheer beauty of design and colour and who cannot promise to make a "scientific" study in connection with them are considerable : special permits, sometimes personal recommendations are necessary to be allowed to handle them.

All the more welcome is an exhibition like the one now open in the Palazzo Venezia in Rome. The moment I heard of its being planned and prepared by Professor Salmi and his assistants I decided to devote several weeks to it, and by good luck on my arrival in Rome, the date of official inauguration having been unexpectedly postponed, I was granted the privilege of being admitted every morning into it, of being seated comfortably before an open case and of being allowed to turn the pages of the codices I wanted to see at my own pace and leisure. Signora Arcamone Barletta could not have been more helpful and hospitable, and my thanks go to her and to her staff for the intense enjoyment I have had, seeing again what I remembered but dimly and finding new treasures. This exhibition affords an opportunity to art students and art lovers not likely to occur soon again of getting acquainted with what is as a rule hidden away in the public, private and ecclesiastical libraries of Italy. In fact, the title of " Mostra Storica Nazionale della Miniatura " does not seem to me well chosen. It should rather have been " Mostra dei Tesori delle Biblioteche Italiane " in view of the many highly interesting codices, Byzantine, Carolingian, Mudejar, northern generally of the Romanesque, Gothic and Renaissance periods not grown on Italian soil, that we find among the exhibits. But I daresay the present title is more attractive and exciting for the general public. In any case it is a magnificent show and does great honour to those who have planned and prepared it.

I cannot in the limited space at my disposal expatiate on the quality of the books exhibited and will only mention some of the more outstanding ones. For instance, the whole series of the Southern Italian Exultet Rolls exhibited in a room by themselves, naïve and yet at times gorgeously decorative scrolls of the XIth, XIIth and XIIIth centuries with the text and notes to be read by the deacon who chanted them while the Easter candle was being lit and the paintings in the opposite sense could be seen by the congregation (Plates 61, 62). For reasons unknown to me both these scrolls and the elaborately carved stands for the Easter candle, like the ones still to be seen at Gaeta, Capua, Sessa Aurunca, Ravello (to mention only the most famous ones), seem to have been used till the XIIIth century only (Plate 63).

Another codex which for years I had been longing to see is the Codex Purpureus Rossånensis, along with the fragmentary Codex Sinopensis in Paris, among the most revealing as well as most beautiful productions of late Antique, and not yet Byzantine art (Plate 64). Fairly good reproductions of it exist, it is true, and my library owns them, but again and again my plans for getting to Rossano in order to examine the original had been frustrated. More than forty years ago, on our way back from Sicily with Carlo Placci in a small car driven by Carlo's nephew Lucien Henraux, we decided to make the then very difficult deviation from Cosenza to Rossano and sent Carlo's Sicilian valet Giuseppe ahead by train to make arrangements about food and lodging. On the highroad where the road turns off to Rossano we found him waiting for us in a state of frantic excitement. He assured us that Rossano was a real robbers' nest, that he had fled from it in order to warn us in good time not to approach it and not to attempt any night's rest or even meal there. Placci, much impressed, refused to go any further and we were obliged to retrace our steps. I suspect that Giuseppe, quite a Don Juan in his own line, had got into trouble with a Calabrian beauty or rather with her *fidanzato* and that it was he who was in mortal danger and not we.

During my quiet and so enjoyable mornings in the magnificent rooms of the Palazzo Venezia it amused me to recall the struggles, the disappointments, the almost comic adventures I have been through in the effort to see certain famous illuminated manuscripts. When the learned Monsieur Omont was at the head of the Bibliothèque Nationale in Paris he seemed to rejoice sadistically in making it almost too wearisome for human patience to try to see the treasures of which he was the jealous guardian. Frightened assistants would invariably assure one that what one wanted was *à la reserve* and impossible to see without M. Omont's special permission. Only by wasting much time did I manage to get the better of the grand eunuch and could see and even enjoy all I wanted. The word eunuch recalls harems and the most famous of all at Yildiz Kiosk, the former residence of the Sultans at Constantinople. I was most anxious to see a Byzantine octateuch in its library and finally the Superintendent of Fine Arts came in person to show it, but also to make sure that nothing else, none of the marvellous Islamic codices nor a number of Titianesque portraits of Sultans, were shown to me. *Une petite Turquitude,* as the great Hamdi Bey would have said, the elder brother of the Superintendent in question.

I remember vividly visits to libraries in Germany soon after the first world war. I was perhaps thoughtless to expect " intellectuals ", always more emotional about politics than soldiers or business men, to receive hospitably a citizen of a power that had helped to defeat their country. For instance, being an assiduous reader of Eduard Meyer's historical writings, I inquired in Berlin whether I could pay my respects to their author. The rough answer came that he would not touch the hand of an enemy alien. Finding myself in Braunschweig I drove out to the library of Wolfenbuettel. It attracted me in the first place because Lessing had been its director, and Lessing, who more than anyone else has started our way of thinking about art, was a saint in my calendar. And then the library contained a number of early manuscripts I was eager to see.

I entered and asked to see the librarian. A pleasant young man said he was coming presently but what could he do for me meanwhile.

I gave him the numbers of the codices I wanted
to see. He looked embarrassed and hesitating,
but invited me to sit down and said he would
bring them. I had scarcely opened the first
volume when he came again, red in the face and
almost trembling, and said his chief had arrived
and wanted to see me at once in his private study.
There I found a brutal-looking Nordic purple
with rage who yelled at me, wanting to know
who I was, what I had come for, how I dared,
who recommended me. I tried to tell him, but
his Berserker *Jaehzorn*—the mad rage of Nordic
heroes—kept increasing till I saw there was
nothing doing and that it was better to leave him
to indulge his fury alone. It must have been
roused by the sight of my car before the door, an
Italian one and to him the symbol of the trium-
phant victory.

On the same trip I wanted to see the library
of Aschaffenburg. It was pouring with rain and
I sent the car for the librarian. It came back
without him. He refused to take advantage of
an enemy car. Then an elderly man under an
umbrella appeared, and full of indignation asked
for my passport and wanted to know why I had
helped to defeat his country. I answered that
I had little to do with it but that it was getting

late and if he would not show me the manuscripts I would leave at once. Grudgingly he consented, let me in and began with the famous Maximilian Codex. Gradually as he watched me looking and heard me commenting he started cooling down and the longer we looked together the more softspoken he became. Finally he kept begging me to stay on as there was so much more to see.

An admirable trait in Germans of all classes, the highest and the lowest, army commanders as well as sacristans and museum guards, is their helpfulness the moment they perceive that one really cares and understands.

To return to the main object of this short article, the exhibition in the Palazzo Venezia, let me express the hope that a way may be found of keeping it open at least for six months and that libraries, cathedrals and private owners will be ready to make the sacrifice of being deprived of their treasures, thus enabling the greatest possible number of specialists, art lovers and cultivated tourists to visit it. I for my part would even advocate the creation of a museum of illuminated manuscripts so as to integrate these precious codices into the history of art along with all other paintings. Through the miraculous preservation

of their colour they should supplement what
has been lost in panel and fresco painting
instead of being treated as mere appendage like
other minor arts.

I Tatti
Settignano
January 1954

XI

EXHIBITIONITIS

About a month ago I had a disheartening
account from a Parisian friend of the exhibition
of Venetian Masterpieces at the Orangerie. She
said the pictures looked " damp, frozen, and
like toys in a shop ".

The same day I read in the *Corriere della Sera*
bits from Ugo Ojetti's diary of 1929. He desig-
nates me as the *ferocissimo* Berenson because I
opposed the kicking about of Italy's finest panel
paintings from here to Paris, from Paris to
London, from London to New York, and thence
to all sorts of midwestern and western towns of
the United States. At one moment the ship that
carried them nearly foundered. They came
back, but few of us have seen in exactly what
condition they were when unpacked. Obvious
damage may seldom appear. The visible harm
may be nothing like so serious as what happens
inside of these paintings, composed as they are

of organic matter still to some extent alive, yet having found a *modus vivendi* between the warring elements so long as they remained in the same hygrometric as well as thermometric conditions and, of course, in more or less the same lighting. Two instances among many jump to my mind. The last time I was at Montpellier I looked for the *Deposition* by Lambert Lombard and could not find it at first, where I remembered it, hanging high up on the wall. Looking down, I saw it lying in fragments on the floor. Horrified, I asked what had happened and was told that the picture had not been moved for generations, had been taken down to be sent to an exhibition at Antwerp and in the course of the night, moved from its habitat, it burst into pieces. Another case is what happened to one of Titian's two Bacchanales, which were sent to be shown at Geneva in 1939. I could not find it in the exhibition and asked why. I was taken to a basement and saw the painting completely detached from its sustaining canvas. In this particular case it was, however, a price worth paying as the Geneva exhibition meant saving the Prado pictures from the danger of destruction by war.

I am not opposed to exhibitions on principle.

Between 1890 and 1914, at a time when photographs were scarce and reproductions poor, when owing to difficult communications many things remained inaccessible and there was still so much to learn in a rudimentary way, I recall exhibitions that were real eye-openers. The New Gallery Exhibition in London (1893), the exhibition of Sienese Art in Siena (1904), the Exhibition of Umbrian Art in Perugia (1907), and particularly the great exhibition of Muslim Art in Munich (1910) belonged to that category, and, among the more recent ones, let me mention the exhibition of Ferrarese Painting at Ferrara in 1933. I still retain a feeling of warm gratitude to the exhibition in Barcelona some twenty-five years ago of the finest treasures, either inaccessible or too jealously guarded in churches and monasteries all over the Iberian Peninsula. Illuminated Manuscripts can be exhibited, as now in the Palazzo Venezia, without running too great a risk and to everybody's advantage. So can *objets d'art* of every kind.

Living artists must have fairs in which annually and bi-annually or every four years they can display the creations of their genius. Neophytes not too sure of their own originality, need hospices to shelter them.

It is the Old Masters, particularly when painted on panel, that with every year that passes tend to become more vulnerable and should be treated with greater care. Instead of which, these *Grands Invalides* are increasingly obliged to change habits and to go travelling. And what about those who make a pilgrimage to see a masterpiece and find its shrine empty?

So much for possible and probable damage to pictures. There is, perhaps, an even more serious consideration. It is the confusion produced in the minds of spectators, most of them lacking visual convictions and untrained in the appreciation of works of art, by having all sorts and kinds of artifacts and works of art cast before them. Here in Italy, the infantile, emergent, incunabulistic products, from the most barbarous and most savage parts of the world, have been seldom shown. But for the over-powering influence of Paris it is doubtful whether Italian artists, left to themselves, would have taken to daubing the way so many of them do.

In Paris the uninterrupted rotation of exotic objects from every part of the earth has ended first in confusing and then in destroying faith in the correspondence between what people usually saw with their own eyes and the way artists reproduced them in painting and sculpture. It encouraged the fumbling, the criss-crossing, the " deformation ", the infantilism of the last thirty or forty years. These more and more alienating departures from our civilized normal visualization have ended logically in ignoring the seen object altogether and in the fervid cult of non-representational and finally in abstract painting.

I recall a beautiful summer day before the first world war in Paris when, walking down the spacious steps of the Grand Palais, I said to a friend : " This exhibition of *Art Nègre* will start a return to savagery just as the Italian Renaissance was a return to the Antique."

The appeal of this kind of art to young artists is easily understood. The toil and moil and sweat required to mature an artist of the traditional schools was chiefly in learning to draw. The practice of to-day ignores drawing altogether. All you have to do to be an artist is to load a brush with paint and swish it. No doubt it gives the artist of to-day great muscular satisfaction.

What the public gets out of it is beyond my charitable understanding and I refuse to indulge the uncharitable explanations that arise in me over the enthusiasm of the intelligentsia.

To return to the exhibitions of Old Masters, there too I ask what even a cultivated public gets out of them. They are too crowded to invite, indeed they all but prevent, the kind of contemplation that leads to feeling and understanding. They encourage mere curiosity and the idle flitting from one work to another. It ends in a vague sense of having seen something they can talk about for a day or two and the satisfaction of having done what one must do to be up to date and " in it ".

This is surely the case with the exhibitions of the obscurer artists which serve chiefly to facilitate the rapid summations of young attributors and critics. To them, what do they yield but the crudest information, the kind Heine poked fun at 125 years ago when in his *Bagni di Lucca* he pillories a snob who boasted of knowing who painted every picture in a gallery and when it was done. Information by itself, which these shows encourage, seldom leads to knowledge and knowledge alone rarely to understanding.

The mania for exhibitions goes so far that nearly every town drags its pictures and other movable objects from where they can be enjoyed separately to dump them down at a show. One enterprising person wanted to exhibit all of Fra Angelico's paintings, which would have necessitated the transfer of that artist's works from San Marco, the Uffizi and Pitti to the Palazzo Strozzi.

Artists in the past did not paint and carve with the idea of a one-man-show (and, of course, not of museums either). They worked to order as a rule and, although the product was seen by friends and enemy-friends, nobody dreamt of exhibiting them to the world at large and against entrance fees.

Small service is done to attractive but not outstanding artists by bringing together the greater part of their movable works and showing them off in a rather theatrical way. Taken out of their accustomed surroundings they lose in quality and produce a confusing and almost exasperating effect.

My conclusion is that exhibitions rarely serve the ultimate justification of the work of art, which is to help the spectator to become a work of art himself.

I Tatti
Settignano
February 1954

XII

WISHFUL ATTRIBUTIONS

" What's in a name ? That which we call a
rose by any other name would smell as sweet
. . ." yes, so it would if the other name called
up the same rosy sensations, the same memories
of rose-ness, the same emotions and above all
the same expectations ; in short, if the other
name affected one exactly as did the first. The
same thing happens with works of art and
especially with visual products : painting, sculpture and even architecture.

I am here concerned with names in painting.
When I pronounce the words Giotto, Michelangelo, Leonardo, Giorgione, Dürer, Velasquez,
Vermeer, Ingres, Manet, Degas and hundreds of
others, each stands for certain qualities which
I expect to find in a painting ascribed to them.
If the expectation fails, then no argument, no
documentary evidence, be it biographical, historical, psycho-analytical, or radiographical and

chemical, will persuade me. Two or three years
ago I read an article which attempted to prove
by every conceivable argument that a certain
panel was by Duccio, whereas by examining the
photographic reproduction I saw that the panel
could only have been painted by Cimabue.
Recently two canvases in the Borghese Gallery
in Rome have come into the limelight as newly
discovered masterpieces by Giorgione (Plates 65,
66). To my eyes they are neither masterpieces
nor by Giorgione, but by one of that lyrical
artist's operatic followers ; possibly Domenico
Caprioli, as Professor Fiocco suggested some
years ago.[1]

It is not my intention to wash in public the
dirty linen of us *connoisseurs* of painting. I would
rather say a few words about the universal
tendency to ascribe a given work of art to the
greatest artist to whom wishful thinking and
excited imagination can ascribe it. What have
I not come across sailing under the flag of Giotto,
of Leonardo, of Raphael, of Correggio, of
Giorgione ! Any sturdy powerful figure would
be attributed to Giotto, any simpering and rather

---

[1] To my surprise I find that as long ago as 1897 I myself
attributed these two " Caricatured Heads " to Caprioli
in the Third Edition of my *Venetian Painters*.

equivocal face to Leonardo, any pretty one to Raphael (*belle comme une Madonne de Raphael*), any amorous face to Correggio, any leathery face decked with plumage to Giorgione. I have seen German late XVIIth-century paintings on copper labelled with one or other of these names. What leads people to make these wild attributions?

In the past there was ignorance. The few names I have mentioned were the only familiar ones, not only out of Italy but in Italy itself. When young I was invited to a patrician house in Verona, and asked what I was about? I answered : " Studying the old masters." " Old masters ! " exclaimed the presiding lady, " we know only the divine Raphael." Which reminded me of a passage in Oliver Goldsmith's *Vicar of Wakefield* in which the Vicar's vagabond son tells of meeting a cousin in Paris who appears to be making a good livelihood by " collecting pictures, medals, intaglios and antiques of all kinds for a gentleman in London ". When asked " how he had been taught the art of the *cognoscente* so suddenly ", he assured the Vicar's son " that nothing was more easy. The whole secret consisted in a strict adherence to two rules : the one always to observe that the picture might have been better if the painter had taken more pains, and the other to praise the works of Pietro Perugino."

A name was then a category. Anything remotely recalling the category was attached to the name. Only a few days ago I came across a charming volume, recently re-published, of *Harriet Beaujolais Campbell's Diary in Florence in 1817*, and found in it amusing proof of the Augean stable that XVIIIth- and early XIXth-century connoisseurship was. She describes her visit to the Academy and the pictures seen there : " in the one by Andrea Varrochio [*sic*] the subject of which was the Baptism of Christ, Ludovico Carracci painted one of the angels. The master was so hurt with seeing how far he was surpassed by his own scholar that he would not suffer him to continue."

Nowadays, after all the work done by Cavalcaselle, Morelli and their successors, there is little excuse for the wild attributions still being made.

One can understand the dealers, the amateur merchants and collectors speculating for a rise ; but why should art historians and gallery directors do the same ? Surely they are not actuated by sordid motives of gain, nor to any extent by questions of prestige.

I suspect that every familar name liberates a specific emotion of enthusiastic love or passionate hate. In the case of the great masters it can only be love. By bestowing a name on a work of art we englobe that work in all the love that it arouses in us and at the same time shut our eyes to the elements which, seen dispassionately, make it improbable that the work should be by the artist by whom we hypnotize ourselves into believing it was painted. From multiple experience I know how hypnotizing and blinding it is to concentrate too long on a problem of attribution. One easily tends to exclude adverse factors ; readily accepts any suggestion which may feed our so innocent and praiseworthy desire to add still another masterpiece to those already known, so that public admiration and outpourings of communal enthusiasm may be aroused.

What happens to our evaluation of a great master whose name should be as " a guarded mount ", when novelty and excitement have ceased to move us, and attribution is based on mediocre flimsy works *à la maniere de* ? Surely the Giorgione (to take an example) who painted the queer things now attributed to him by many writers is scarcely worth the fame, the admiration and the love even, that we gave him when we accepted only the ten or twelve works allocated to him by Giovanni Morelli.

Oscar Wilde used to say : " we end by killing the thing we love ". By loving too much the name of a great painter and bestowing it on mediocre and even vulgar works of art we dim his fame, diminish his value and reduce him to the rank of an unequal practitioner who had, it is true, moments of inspiration, but was often too disappointing to call out our admiration and affection.

POSTSCRIPT
TO WISHFUL ATTRIBUTIONS

It happens, on the other hand, that we cannot help inserting a picture on morphological and technical grounds into the *opus* of a great master, but it would be foolish to exalt it because of the name it carries. Not only Homer nods once in a while. All artists do and not infrequently. One of the ablest painters and best portraitists of the years before the flood that has overwhelmed us, the German Max Liebermann, used to say : " We artists owe you attributors a real debt for relieving us of our mediocre and even stupid efforts." No artist's works are invariably up to the best. We must not idealize and expect too much from poor human nature, not even from its most gifted children. Leonardo is capable of painting the Benois Madonna of the Hermitage, a young woman with a senile grin, Raphael can be cloying, Correggio over-sensual. Giorgione in his Glasgow *Christ and the Adulteress* fringes on vulgarity. Not only in the field of visual art. The same with literature and music. Where is the writer who does not get prolix and boring ? Even a Beethoven thumps and bangs. We must admit these moments of weakness on the part of genius itself, and not go into ecstasies over a work that for adequate reasons we are obliged to ascribe to a great artist.

We should admire and cherish the work of art for its intrinsic qualities and not because of its attribution to a great artist. The rationalizer and reformer of connoisseurship, Giovanni Morelli, used to cite in Bergamask dialect a saying that I quote from memory in Italian : " Chi guarda cartello non mangia vitello."

I Tatti
Settignano
March 1954

XIII

FOR WHOM ART

And He said unto them : The Sabbath was made for man and not man for the Sabbath.   Mark 2, 27.

With due reverence I venture to use this sacred text for a lay sermon on the relation of art to man.

Artists in all realms of art, verbal, visual, musical, writers, whether critics of what is going on to-day or historians of what has been done in the past, tend now as never before to ignore the public that can enjoy the work of art and by enjoying assimilate it and be on the way to become itself a work of art.

The versifier of to-day expects to be admired not by a public brought up to enjoy poetry but only by other versifiers and their academic applauders.   No outmoded nonsense about rapture, about ecstasy, about longing, yearning, about *la vallée de larmes où il fait si bien de pleurer.* No music, no readily felt rhythm, no rhyme, scarcely any appeal to the ear.   Some versifiers go so far as to proclaim that they write for the eye and the eye only.

Music of recent years to a mere listener who like me has been a lifelong lover of music—the most man-made, the most transporting of all the arts—sounds shrill, strident, banging, booming, scraping. Composers of the last thirty years write for each other logically disharmonized compositions, stuffed with newness as a sausage is of meat.

As for the visual arts (my own occupation and preoccupation for the last seventy years), they now seem to be practised by individuals who have something to hide or to run away from. If they represent objects at all, they besmirch and bedaub and pull them out of shape as if they dared not exhibit them plain. Why this concealment unless they are afraid of showing up as poor draughtsmen? Is it because they despair of being able to draw at all? Or because like Picasso and his like they want to impress each other by exhibits of virtuoso dexterity, by indulging in acrobatics, in changes as seasonal as those of dressmakers?

Where does the public come in, the cultivated public to which we belong, the same public that hitherto expected the artist to give shape to things, to enhance, to interpret, to fix aspirations, yearnings, dreams? It asks for bread and is given not even a stone.

We, the public, exist only to pay with our purses and to bleat in the chorus of praise, gratitude and worship that the artist, always a genius, now expects from our humility.

The writers about art ignore the public almost as flagrantly. They are of two kinds. Those who serve as a claque for the artists of to-day and those who study the artists of the past—a past stretching back thousands of years.

Neither the one nor the other has many if any words to say about what the work of art should mean to us. Value is ignored. For the art critic, the talk seldom if ever is what the product of to-day does for us and to us. He expatiates on the technical achievements as if addressing himself to painters or sculptors. Why does he do it? They surely have no need of his kind instruction. They know their trade as he does not, even if he has been too incompetent as painter or sculptor to go on with the craft and in despair turns to writing about it. Perhaps they lack the sense of aesthetic values and do not know what to do about a new work of art, but to repeat the approval, the mutterings, the gossip

E.A.—H

of the studio. Such information is of small
interest to the rest of us unless the critic is gifted
enough to turn what he writes into a work of
literary art that we can enjoy for its own sake, as
we do what Delacroix, what Fromentin, and
what, on another level, Zola, Ojetti, Valéry,
Vollard have written.

When not writing about the still living or
recently deceased artist's specific technique, the
critic of the last decades becomes psycho-analyst,
metaphysician, mystogogue in his effort to explain why a given painter has driven his brush
backward and forward, why he displaces eyes,
why he duplicates and triplicates noses in profiles
and commits other mutilations on " the human
face divine ". The only result is that with a
person like me, with my seventy years' experience
of visual art, his writings are as unintelligible,
as confusing, as mystifying as the pictures and
sculptures he tries to justify. I want to ask *qui
trompe-t-on ici* ?

So much for the critics who write about what
is being done in their day and hour. The art
historians of recent years have as little regard
for the public. They rarely start with an appreciation of the object in question, about its value
as a work of art, what it should do to the onlooker,

what it should mean to him ; whether sufficiently life-enhancing to be worth while or
merely a microscopic fact delighting in the
researcher and the researcher only.

Here too the cultivated public who should
ask for the bread of aesthetic enjoyment is given
the sand of research, wrangles about attributions,
displays of scholastic erudition and dialectics.
Art historians unintentionally exaggerate the
importance of the artist they are studying and
give an aesthetic value to his works that I for one
fail to perceive in them. Paolo Uccello, for
instance, because of his life-absorbing excitement
over perspective, ranks now as an artist of the
highest order, which he is but seldom. Likewise
Castagno, a swaggering decorator and over-
expressive illustrator, is now esteemed by art
historians of the expressionistic school above the
greatest genius of the Florentine mid-Quattro-
cento, Antonio Pollaiuolo.

We are living in an age when quantitative
science, machinery and a somewhat shy hankering
for metaphysics dominate all thought and writing,
as Evolution did after Darwin and *milieu* after
Buckle. The prevailing problem in all fields of
art is of " how " always, of " why " sometimes,
of " what " never.

Burckhardt and Woelfflin always used to begin
an essay on an artist or a given work of art by
drawing the reader's attention to all significant
details and to interpret them in terms of their
appeal to our hearts, our minds, our souls. Few
if any of us do so now.

We plunge immediately into every kind of not
too relevant consideration of who the artist was
in private life, who his parents, cousins and aunts,
what wives, mistresses and concubines he had,
who was his very first master, who his primary
school teacher. Then come wrangles over dates
and questions of priority. For instance, did
Michelangelo do certain chisel-strokes on the
12th or the 15th of May, 1527? Who was the
first to invent this or that motive? What precise
technique did the painter use? What people
did the poet or composer meet, what emotional
crisis was he suffering while creating in verse,
in prose, in music?

Such interests, occupations and preoccupations
take us away from the one and only thing that is
of vital importance in connection with the work
of art and its creator, namely to interpret and
communicate. Finding it difficult, writers tend
to treat art as a pedantic job, or follow the
fashion of expatiating on " how " and " why "

and scarcely ever on " what ". Their *parole* is,
" Away with Art ".

Surely it is time that we rebelled and cried :
A chi l'Arte ?   A noi ! [1]

I Tatti
Settignano
April 1954

[1] Parody of the early Fascist battle-cry, *A chi l'Italia?
A noi !*—For whom Italy ?   For us !

XIV

NOTES ON GIORGIONE

I had spent the greater part of a year playing patience with ordinary and X-ray photos of every painting attributed to Giorgione in the last sixty years. I did the same with all known pictures that can be classified as Giorgionesque. I had meant to write a book, a comprehensive book on the subject. At the end I realized that it would take me another year to do the kind of book I had in mind, and that I had no time to spare for it. Besides, I ended by doubting whether I had much to publish that others would not do as well. I would leave many problems not only unsettled but not more advanced toward a satisfactory solution.

At the same time a lancing suspicion of the uselessness of arguing about attributions and datings overcame me. I have waded through such swamps of argument to reach with my own eye conclusions opposite to those so minutely laboured by the writer. My present conviction is that what counts in the art of attribution is not this or that minute comparison but a sense of the painter's artistic personality. That sense comes only after a long and loving intimacy and by no short cuts. And least of all by comparing minutiae of questionable significance.

So I have abandoned the idea of composing a ponderous work on Giorgione. Instead, to honour my ever-helpful colleague and dear friend, Giuseppe Fiocco, I publish a short note on the *Old Woman " Col Tempo "* in the Venice Academy, and an attempt to find out who was the painter of the Oxford and Leningrad Madonnas ascribed by some students to Giorgione himself.

THE GIPSY OF THE ''TEMPESTA'' AND THE OLD WOMAN ''COL TEMPO''

The attribution to Giorgione of the Old Woman with the words " Col Tempo " (Plate 67) is now beyond need of proof. It would be enough to place it side by side with the Gipsy of the *Tempesta* (Plate 68) for the trained eye to see that they were by the same artist.

I should like to say a few words of another kind about the two. It is my belief that they were painted at about the same time, as indeed is manifested by the identical folds of kerchief and tunic in both. I would go further and fancy that the artist imagined how the woman who had served as model for the Gipsy would look *col tempo* as an old woman. Nearly the same dome-shaped cranium, nearly the same high forehead, same parting and dropping to sides of the hair, features, eyes, nose, cheeks, chin sufficiently alike. All has undergone a sad change. The brow and cheeks are furrowed and wrinkled, the eyes bleary and gummy, the mouth oozing through broken teeth, the throat leathery, the expression one of physical discomfort, of distress even.

Giorgione was certainly under thirty when he painted this old woman and probably five or six years younger. Even if he had a model for accurate rendering of details, a concept of old age so complete, so convincing could have been entertained only by a creative imagination of the highest order.

I feel tempted to let my fancy run free, and to weave the plot of a romance around these two pictures, the *Soldier and Gipsy* or *Tempesta* and the

Old Woman " Col Tempo ". The soldier would be the young Giorgione himself looking on while the somewhat more mature woman was giving suck to his and her child. She may be suffering a revulsion of feeling against him for having brought her to this pass, and he painted her as she would look when old, as an admonition to gather roses while she might for time was aflying.

THE GIORGIONESQUE HERMITAGE AND OXFORD MADONNAS

Some years ago the enterprising Ashmolean Museum of Oxford University acquired a *Madonna* which was at once recognized as by the hand that painted another *Madonna* at the Hermitage, and like that attributed by many critics to no less an artist than Giorgione himself (Plates 69, 70).

The object of this short essay is to examine these two works, to look for other paintings by the same hand, and to try to identify that hand.

We begin with the Hermitage *Madonna*, probably the earliest of the series.

The features and expression vaguely recall the woman in Giorgione's *Soldier and Gipsy*, but are a trifle more refined. The Madonna sits beside a pool and bends forward so as to support with

her right hand the restless Child on her lap.
Behind her cliffs and quarries, Bellini-Giorgion-
esque buildings across the pool and distant
mountains. Close at hand Giorgionesque foliage.
The folds of the ample draperies are not Giorgionesque. Yet the atmosphere, the mood recalls
the magician of Castelfranco.

In the Hermitage picture the Madonna holds
a closed book in her left hand. In the Ashmolean
painting (Plate 69) the identical left hand with
the help of the right holds open the book in
which she is reading, and the Child in sharp
profile looks up at her as he reclines cushioned
on the parapet. Beyond a second parapet
closing in a garden, a memory view of Piazzetta,
Doge's Palace, Campanile, etc. The Virgin's
face is rounder, the nose more angular, the body
more massive than in the Hermitage picture, the
folds of draperies more sweeping and more linear,
particularly over the knees.

Let us sum up the results of what we have seen
in these two pictures. They are manifestly by
the same hand, they are Giorgionesque. In its
linear draperies the Hermitage picture is less
Giorgionesque than the Ashmolean one. Also we
have an indication of when the last was done in
the fact that the Campanile is still without its

pyramidal top as it remained till 1510. If by a
resident of Venice surely not before, and if a
memory picture scarcely much later than 1510
seeing how constant were the communications
between Venice and its dependencies.

Was the author of these two Madonnas
Giorgione himself? Let us see what other
paintings, in all probability by the same hand,
have to tell us.

I confess that it would be desirable to find a
connecting link between the last two works and
those that now will be examined. Some day
the inconsiderable hiatus may be filled. At
present it may require some effort to recognize
the same hand in the Madonna with Saint
Catherine and the Baptist of the Venice Accademia (Plate 71). Features by features, in
pose, in expression, the Virgin is scarcely more
different from the last two than they from each
other, but the folds of her draperies are more
functional, more linear, more smoothly flowing,
more decidedly Giorgionesque. She sits against
a creased curtain as in the Oxford picture. Her
hands are placed in exactly the same way,
although their shape is smoothed out. Saint
John's hand, however, is more like those in the
Hermitage and Ashmolean works. The Child

is little changed from the one in the last-mentioned picture. The Saint Catherine may be a portrait with hand and features taken from life, but the folds of her draperies are of the same character as the Virgin's.

The next work is a Madonna belonging to Signor Viezzoli of Genoa (Plate 72). In some ways she is near to the Hermitage Madonna in type and pose and in the folds of her left arm. Indeed, she is closer to the Ashmolean Madonna, but the sweep of her mantle, the Child, the hands seem more advanced than in the Venice picture.

I would follow with a Madonna in the London National Gallery (No. 2495, Plate 73). The nose is sharper than in the Ashmolean Madonna. The Child looks up at her as in that picture, but he reclines and points to his mouth as in the Genoese Madonna. The hands of the National Gallery Virgin and the Genoese one are identical. The colouring (as I remember it) is like Palma's in that Master's middle period.

There is yet another work that seems to be by the same hand. It is a large painting in the Galleria Nazionale of the Barberini Palace (No. 618, Plate 74) and represents the Madonna sewing while she and Saint Elizabeth look happily at the infant Jesus and infant Baptist playing with flowers and with a lamb. Elizabeth is older but in every way identical with the National Gallery Madonna. The draperies have points of significant similarity with the pictures already examined.

Years ago I included this canvas in my *Italian Pictures of the Renaissance* as being by Cariani, and I am more than ever convinced that it is by him.

The blond colouring and technique are characteristic of his Palmesque phase. His are the hill towns and distant mountains. Let us for comparison look at a canvas the attribution of which to Cariani has never been and never can be questioned. It is the *Invention of the Cross* in the Bergamo Gallery (Plate 75). A trifle later and more advanced, it yet has striking resemblances with the Roman picture. Compare the Madonna in the one with the Saint Elizabeth in the other, the Holy children and the Lamb in the Roman painting with those in the Bergamo one. The draperies of the kneeling saint in the last with that of the Saint Elizabeth in the other, and the vaporous distance.

The Cariani we know already hovers rustically between Giorgione and Palma, closer to the latter.

He can be out-and-out Giorgionesque as we see him in one of his most delightful creations in that mode, the Bergamo Nude asleep over his lute and the woman playing (Plate 28). That Cariani was an ardent student of Giorgione we may conclude from his having made a faithful copy (also at Bergamo, Plate VI of Luciano Gallina, Giovanni Cariani) of the Glasgow *Adulteress*.

The conclusion may be startling, but I do not see how it can be avoided. The Hermitage and Oxford pictures as well as the other paintings that go with them are early works by Cariani.

I Tatti
Settignano
July 1954

XV

GUIDO RENI

The young—*les Jeunes*—are rediscovering Guido Reni. I for one had never forgotten him. In my first years in Rome dating from 1888, Guido's *Aurora* in the Palazzo Rospigliosi was one of the most frequented and admired of works of art, as much as the Sixtine Chapel or the Stanze of Raphael. Early in this century the cult of the Primitifs came to a head. It had been started a hundred years earlier by the German Wackenroder and his countrymen, the " Nazarener " painters in Rome. What a pity that critics seem incapable of enjoying a new admiration without jeering at what went before. So Guido and Domenichino and many others were almost forgotten and nobody looks at the Aurora any more. Indeed, it is no longer accessible to the public.

It was an excellent idea of the Bolognese civic authorities and scholars to revive interest in Guido

Reni by bringing together most of his movable
paintings in an admirably arranged exhibition
and to supply a publication that not only reproduces all the exhibits, not only furnishes a catalogue where each item is fully discussed, but
contains a subtle and illuminating appreciation
by Professor Gnudi of Guido the artist, followed
by a chronological account of his life and career,
and completed with an extensive biography. The
catalogue, in short, is a handbook, indeed an
encyclopedia of genuine information regarding
the master such as few other artists enjoy. It
even reproduces a fair number of Guido's
drawings.

Now let me try to put down in words the
impression left on me by this display of Guido's
works and the conclusions I have attempted to
reach regarding his rank as artist.

In the first place he is a remarkable composer,
but a theatre composer rather than as Raphael a
wall decorator. His *Massacre of the Innocents* of
the Bologna Gallery (Plate 76), his *Samson with
the Jawbone of an Ass*, also at Bologna (Plate 77),
his *Archangel Michael* of the Cappuccini in Rome
(Plate 78), his *Atalanta and Hippomene* from Naples,
his *Sacred and Profane Love* from Pisa are arrangements of lines crossed and recrossed, of masses

carefully balanced, of figures and personages orchestrated, so to speak, with surroundings of noble architecture and fabulously effective low sea-horizons. They call up highly elaborated effects on the stage just before the curtain comes down. Far be it from me to admire Guido less for all this, nor is he in the bad sense of the word theatrical, but it is well to observe how his compositions seldom suggest reposeful conclusions as those due to artists of previous generations and as, for instance, his own majestic *Giving of the Keys to Peter* at Perpignan (Plate 79).

As an illustrator his best qualities are displayed in the works already mentioned and supremely in the so evocative and radiant *Aurora* of the Rospigliosi in Rome, as well as in the chapel of the Quirinal and at San Gregorio Magno in Rome again. He fails lamentably in the *Rape of Helen* at the Louvre and many of his pictures are spoiled by the presence of a distressed but icy female copied from the late-antique Niobe. His altarpieces and other religious paintings are apt to be over-expressive in intention and unconvincing and empty in result.

Exceptions, perhaps because not done with pietistic intent, are the so attractive young Apollo of Dulwich (Plate 80), recognizable as the youthful

Baptist only by his staff ending in a cross, and the altogether admirable picture of the Girolamini at Naples representing the *Meeting of the adolescent Jesus and the young Baptist* (Plate 81). The look of wonder, of submission, of humility on the part of the latter as he is received by the Apollinian figure of the youthful Jesus is as convincing and as moving as any other representation known to me. I cannot help being reminded of Velasquez' *Lanzas* where the Dutch general and Spinola have the same relation and nearly the same expression. One may legitimately ask whether Velasquez had not seen this work and whether the vague recollection of it may not have helped him to compose his great masterpiece.

Is this, I wonder, the only reminder of Guido in Velasquez' paintings ? The portrait of a pope from Corsham Court representing Clement VIII (as that devoted *aficionado* of the late Bolognese, Mr. Denis Mahon, proposes) may have been known to the great Spaniard (Plate 82). In composition, in pose it is so startlingly like his Innocent X of the Doria Palace. They are not to be compared for quality of painting, but as studies of character surely Guido is in no way inferior. His pope is psychologically incomparably more interesting. Instead of the plethoric, sanguine, overripe animal that we find in Innocent X we have here a subtly thoughtful, disabused, elderly human being resigned to his lot. It makes me think of another magnificent portrait of Renis, a cardinal seated with a curtain behind him and a landscape to the left seen through a colonnade. It used to belong to the Wimbornes and was sold at auction at Christie's in 1923 for the modest sum of 80 guineas (Plate 83).

There are other portraits claiming attention. Two in the Bologna Gallery, one of an elderly woman anxious to do good, almost too good, convincingly characterized and beautifully drawn (Plate 84), the other supposed to represent the artist's mother, an even subtler and more detailed study of anxiety and good intention painted as well as the pictorial language of Bologna of that time could achieve (Plate 85). Similar to the first as psychological interpretation is the bust of an old man I saw years ago in Mr. David Erskine's collection in Scotland (Plate 86). Finally, there is the portrait of himself, unexpectedly jaunty, cavalier-like, reminding one of Van Dyck's *Charles I* of the National Gallery in London.

His colour is brilliant and at times locally

beautiful, but seldom fused and warm as with the Venetians, tending on the contrary to be spotty and glossy almost as in the stone mosaics over the altars of Saint Peter's in Rome. It is colour like a grate with no fire. Only in his later years does it get less sheeny, warmer, with a tendency to monochrome as in the grave and distinguished *Lot and His Daughters* from a private collection in Bologna, the most classical treatment of this curious subject I can recall.

With all these qualities so outweighing any faults hitherto touched upon, why have we in the last fifty or sixty years ceased to care for him the way previous generations did ? And I venture to prophesy that *les Jeunes* of to-day will not succeed in restoring him to the admiration we used to give him. Why, in short, is Guido no longer among the great ? Had he lived around 1500 he might have been. He might have learned to use his imagination of muscular movement and to give grip and tension and relaxation to the personages represented in action. He communicates nothing but the concept in shape of the outlines of limbs and extremities, leaving them dangling without gripping, without pressing, without clinging, without relaxing, without weighing. The result is that Guido represents but seldom presents and fails to communicate an evocation or more than a scene. He scarcely ever makes us forget, for no matter how brief a moment, that we are only looking by making us live and act with the figures in the picture and breathe and walk in the landscape.

If the younger people of to-day refuse to accept my requirements of a work of art, and are satisfied with the husk, I have no means of persuading them. *Chi si contenta gode.*

Bologna
October 1954

XVI

A MONSU' DESIDERIO OF THE QUATTROCENTO

Over a number of years I have been gathering photos of paintings in a portfolio labelled " Frivolous Comparisons ", and meant to publish them some day for my own and my reader's amusement. I never got round to doing it as the time I can devote to my work keeps getting more and more restricted. But to-day, having been invited to contribute a short paper in honour of my dear friend, Lionello Venturi, I am going to dedicate one of these frivolous comparisons to him in the hope that it will entertain him and remind him of our earliest encounters at the time when his work on the Giorgione problem first attracted my attention and admiration.

The painting I want to discuss here is an oblong canvas about two metres wide painted in monochrome. It used to be in England. Recently Count Vittorio Cini has been able to hunt it up and to acquire it for the Castle of Monselice (Plate 87).

The curious thing is that it anticipates the creations of Monsu' Desiderio not only by sub-ordinating the figures to the architecture, but by giving the most fantastic design to the buildings themselves. Three groups of these are combined, of elements jumbled together from mid-Quat-trocento Renaissance, lingering Gothic and sheer vulgar absurdity of the kind committed in the last decade of the XIXth century at Genoa and elsewhere (Plate 88).

Within this fantastical framework we discern, just as in Monsu's paintings, groups of very small figures. They enact scenes from the Pas-sion, beginning with Christ taken to Pilate and ending with the Crucifixion. So subordinated are the figures to the architecture that both Pilate and his wife are but partially visible (Plate 89).

Who this artist could have been I cannot dis-cover. Venetian, certainly, and close follower of Jacopo Bellini.

The costumes would induce one to believe that the picture was painted between 1450 and 1460.

Not far from it, but surely not by the same author, is another monochrome canvas now in Count Vittorio Cini's Collection at Monselice.

I propose it to the attention of fellow students. One or the other may be able to identify the author. I have not succeeded, although I suspect it may have been Bernardino Parenzano in an early and unusually brilliant phase (Plate 90).

First let us look at it. The subject is the Adoration of the Magi. As a composition it recalls Jacopo Bellini, as indeed do the carpentry of the hut, so precise and so fragile, and the garlands of cherubs above the shed. The horsemen descending through the steep ravine, and the strutting *palafreniere* behind the three kings recall Mantegna, of course, and Bartolommeo Vivarini. Here, too, costume would indicate a date between 1450 and 1470. The Oriental in turban carrying a sabre might indicate a connection with Gentile Bellini directly after his return from Constantinople. To our left of the Madonna kneel a man and a woman who may have been donors (Plate 91). Their features are vaguely familiar, but I cannot conjure up from the limbo of memory where I have seen them nor where I have encountered the crowns, one over the other, on the accoutrements of the horses. They may be a device helping to identify the donors and to date the work (Plate 92).

To return to the fantastic and fetching

Desiderio : why was he called " Monsu' " ?
That is and was the Neapolitan title for a *chef*,
for a *cordon bleu* and indeed for any cook of a
noble family. Either Desiderio began active
life in a kitchen or he was the son of a *chef*.
Not impossible that he did start as cook. I once
engaged one who could not cook but made
magnificent architectural pastry.

At the villa of Torre a Cona, beyond San
Donato in Collina to the south-east of Florence,
there is a park filled with statuary of brick and
plaster made by the cook of the great house.
In an inscription he boasts that he is both cook
and sculptor and as proficient in the one as in
the other.

If we knew when the term " Monsu' " for a
cook got current in Naples it might help to give
us Desiderio's still disputed *floruit*.[1]

I Tatti
Settignano
April 1955

[1] In one of the recent numbers of *Paragone* Dr. Raffaello
Causa has published the results of his research work in the
Neopolitan archives on Monsu' Desiderio. He seems to
have settled down in Naples early in the XVIIth century
and to have been called " Monsu' " only on account of,
or because of his being a Frenchman. But there were
hundreds of Frenchmen working in Italy in that period.
Why should none of them have been called Monsu' ?
(1956)

XVII

ENCOUNTERS WITH MATISSE

Soon after 1900 the Stein dynasty began to
hold its court at No. 27 rue de Fleurus. The
founders were Michael and his wife Sally.
When the panting interest in what the youngest
painters were doing was at its full they were
joined by the philosopher brother Leo and by
the sister Gertrude, as yet guiltless of her later
glossolalic triumphs.

I do not recall the private apartments of this
court. The reception hall I remember was long
and narrow like a shed, hung with every kind of
picture done by the youthful painters working in
Paris at that time. In the centre, on a long table
were lined up crisp loaves of bread, cut in half
and stuffed with sausage or ham or meat and in
the middle of the table a large illustrated folio
volume lay open. It was easy to see that the
stuffed loaves were meant to feed the young

aspirants to fame ; but what the folio was doing there I never learnt.

Among the young people I met there the one I recall most clearly was a thick set, vital and gay young Catalan whose name was Picasso. I do not recall seeing at that time any paintings of his, but his drawings struck me as being by a born draughtsman of the highest classical kind already not inferior to Raphael or to Ingres.

Later on there appeared in this hall a bearded, mature, professorial-looking person whose name was Matisse. He talked logically and eloquently of his own attitude to art and in defence of his innovations in pattern and design. He engaged my interest and I went to his studio and saw there the picture representing dancing nudes which to me is still the nearest approach to a great work of art that Matisse ever did (Plate 93). Perhaps my admiration of it was based on my recognizing a curious affinity between it and Pollaiuolo's dancing nudes that a few years before had been discovered in the Torre del Gallo in Florence (Plate 94).

Neither Matisse nor Picasso was earning much and I am confident that the Steins, who bought a number of their things, paid these young men ever so much more than anybody else at that time would have given them for their work. Matisse being already a family man, was, I understand, in serious doubt whether he could go on painting, and Jacques Blanche (*homme du monde*, society portraitist, and the best art critic in Paris at the time) assured me that Matisse was looking for any job that would enable him to live even if it meant being the concierge of some big house.

Some years later, on looking through a number of what was then one of the best English-language weeklies, *The New York Nation*, I found a letter from its Paris correspondent in which the writer spoke of Matisse as a "*fumiste*" who painted "*pour épater le bourgeois*". These current catchwords which the Parisian world applies to every artist before it ends years afterwards in abject adulation of the same artist, irritated me into writing a few words of protest to *The Nation*. Far be it from me to claim that this was the first time Matisse was mentioned in America (or in England), but owing to the fact that I was known to be such a passionate lover of great Classical art, these few words of mine had a startling effect and Gertrude Stein tried to convince me that it was my duty to devote all my energies to making propaganda for Matisse.

Just before the first world war I went to the studio of Matisse with Anne, the daughter of J. P. Morgan, the great New York banker and collector. I found the walls of the studio lined with casts of Cambodian sculpture, and as I looked at his paintings I told him that there were in them too many reminders of Cambodian art. He firmly denied it and when I said " but look at what you have on your walls ! " he either did not know that the casts were of Cambodian reliefs or—what my experience with artists tells me is more likely—he was unaware of having been influenced by them.

As he was still anything but prosperous I wanted to get something from him and I espied a rather rough painting of a forest clearing and asked what he wanted for it. Five hundred francs (gold francs of course) was all he asked and I gave it gladly and carried away the canvas (Plate 95).

I did not see Matisse again for many years. Instinctively I avoid in every walk of life the individual who is having his day. Matisse had meanwhile been recognized as one of the best artists of his time with no rivals except Picasso. Towards the end he too fell under the spell of the Catalan magician and I deplored this subservience and almost lost interest in him.

In 1950, stopping over at Nice on my way back from Paris, it occurred to me to telephone to the great master who was then living at Cimiez. He remembered me and gave me an appointment. I found him living in one of those huge *pueblos* that had been meant before the first world war to serve as an hotel for a wealthy *clientèle* and had subsequently been divided up into big and small apartments. We rang at the door and a handsome, rather severe young Russian woman let us in, made us wait a few minutes and then led us into the presence. While waiting I looked at the white walls. They were scrawled over with huge, heavily drawn bold sketches for the chapel at Vence (Plate 96).

Matisse was lying, or rather sitting up, in a huge bed, bridged over by a wide table on which there was ample room for his drawing material, pencils, charcoal, yellowish paper in abundance. To right and left two revolving bookshelves within reach of his hands. At his feet several fine Angora cats. His look was majestic and benign, very different from the gaunt, perhaps somewhat undernourished face that I first saw nearly fifty years before. I can never resist giving a sharp look at books within the reach of my eyes and I saw that among all those assembled round him there was not a single one that did not speak of him and of his art. He was kindly condescending, *en tres grand seigneur*, spoke of Vence, in his opinion the greatest achievement of his career, mentioned none of the Steins except " Sally ", who was still surviving and established in California. He asked me nothing whatever about myself nor did he refer in the slightest to what I had done for him forty years ago. But he did ask about the landscape I had bought from him, wondering whether I still owned it.

As we got up I noticed in a corner of his room a cast of the ultra-archaic Dion from Athens and a few casts or perhaps originals of south-east Asiatic and Pacific sculpture. As she led us out the young Russian woman showed me with almost religious fervour other rooms, the walls of which were filled with huge sketches for the chapel of Vence.

My conclusion about Matisse is that in the neck-and-neck race with Picasso for the highest place in the art of the last fifty years he ended by coming in second.

Saniet Volpi
Tripoli
May 1955

XVIII

FRA ANGELICO

For sixty years I have been living between Fiesole and Settignano. My tramps on foot would take me as far as Monte Senario, as the slopes of Monte Morello, as the Madonna del Sasso. They got more restricted with the years and are now reduced to a walk downhill from heights which I reach by car.

From all these tramps and walks I looked more or less over the same distances, the same horizon. It ranged from the massif of the Falterona to the Pratomagno, then across the Arno to Monte Scalari, to Miransù, to the Incontro, to San Miniato, to Bellosguardo. Sweeping mountain ranges, tumbled hills, never the majestically elegant views that the word " Italy " conjures up to us Northern Barbarians, so well exemplified by the panorama to be seen from the terrace of the Villa Roti Michelozzi (now Franchetti) at Bellosguardo or from the colonnade of San

Martino alla Palma, that rustic Parthenon, facing the Apennines across the level expanse of the Valdarno before it reaches the narrows of Signa.

Gazing at these landscapes year in year out and in all weathers I kept asking myself why no artist but one ever painted it as I was seeing it, I who have been taught by all the ages of painting.

The Trecento did not look at " Nature ". It improved on the Byzantine heritage and its formulas but never went beyond. The Florentine Quattrocento with few exceptions was too much absorbed in problems of perspective to give more than topographical aspects of nature, exemplified in the achievements of Baldovinetti and Pol- laiuolo and admirable in their own way. Filippo Lippi painted lovely gardens and forest hillsides. Leonardo and his followers offer romantic views and mysterious distances. Of Botticelli, Leon- ardo wrote that all he did to paint a landscape was to throw a sponge dripping with pigment against a panel.

In my own times I have asked French, German, Anglo-Saxon and, needless to say, Italian friends why they did not paint " the Nature " I was trying to make them see. They shrank away and would not touch it.

E.A.—K

One artist did see what I see as I look around me on my walks and even from my windows and that artist was Fra Angelico. Nobody less expected. Knowing as he must have known that the sky looked just as clear to an inhabitant of the far Valdarno as it did to him in Fiesole or in Florence, yet he painted it as he saw it, a pale greyish blue or bluish grey. And equally well he knew that the white spots in the distance corresponded to homesteads, to villas, to churches and painted their geometrical shapes undetailed and looking at the whole as whitish spots in the greyish blue. To use a homely comparison, they seem like white spots of cheese appearing in the whey. One need cite no examples. If you look for them you will find them in any of Angelico's paintings that have distant views in their backgrounds.

He could paint clear skies and romantically clouded skies more evocatively, more convincingly than any of his Italian contemporaries and as well as the great Flemings.

At the same time he portrayed a city scene, the cross-section of a town in a way again unsurpassed by any of his Italian or Flemish contemporaries. His town walls, as in the *Pietà* (Plate 98) and in the great *Deposition* (both in the

San Marco Museum of Florence), are fascinating
creations. They remind me of the long stretches
of town wall at Kairouan (Plate 97 A and B) or at
Sfax. And his view of Jerusalem (Plate 99) with
the temple consisting of diminishing cubes piled
one upon another suggesting a Mesopotamian
Zagaruth—a stepped tower—how did the idea
occur to him? Eastern and Far Eastern notions
may have reached him. Indeed, we have proof
of one instance at least. In the San Marco
altarpiece with many figures surrounding the
enthroned Madonna, Saints Cosmas and Damian
in the foreground kneel on a carpet that must be
from further Asia (Plate 100).

He could render the depth of churches and
other interiors not only with a perfectly satisfactory perspective but with shadows getting
thicker as they get farther and farther away
from the spectator's eye. This effect one
seldom if ever finds in Flemish or other paintings contemporary with Fra Angelico.

Let it not be implied that I admire and love
in Fra Angelico only the quasi-modern painter
of distances, of space, of architecture and town
scenes (Plates 101, 102). I enjoy his celestial
visions inspired to him, as to the illuminators of
Byzantine and German XIIth- and XIIIth-century

purple and golden codices, by descriptions in the Apocalypse of Jerusalem the Golden. I enjoy his gracious visages with their upward look of ecstasy (Plate 103). I enjoy his *naïveté*, his candour, even his occasional doll-like figures. I delight in touches of genre and humour like the woman panting up the hill or the saucy maidservant peeping through the half-shut doors in the Cortona predella panel representing the *Visitation* (Plate 101), a painting already noted for one of the very earliest portrait landscapes in Italian art, a view of Lake Trasimene.

To paint all his panel pictures, all his frescoes at San Marco, in Florence and in the Vatican he must have had a formidable and elaborately organized atelier. He must have had assistants of a high order like the one who for the church of Montecarlo in the upper Valdarno (Plate 107) copied the Annunciation with its predella now at Madrid, or a Madonna like the one from Pontassieve now in the Uffizi. Such was the excellence of the master's training that his pupils got completely identified with him and their individuality disappears without a trace. I for one cannot see in any of the paintings that can be ascribed to Fra Angelico the slightest trace of tenth-rate daubers like Zanobi Strozzi or Domenico di Michelino.

These valuations of Fra Angelico I have held *in petto* for many decades and if I publish them now it is because interest in that great master has flared up after going to exhibitions of his works both in Rome and in Florence.

The entrance cloister of San Marco with the gigantic cedar in its midst on a summer morning is by itself a joy to the eye and all the nobler senses. So are the refectory and the other halls on the ground floor and above all Michelozzo's library upstairs, at last visible in its pristine space effects (Plate 104). It is to the credit of the Florentine *Soprintendenza* to have taken advantage of this occasion for restoring and improving in exemplary fashion the part of the old convent that serves as museum. But I cannot say that the few works brought from outside make Fra Angelico better understood than he is anyway by his masterpieces permanently at San Marco. Besides, it is impossible to appreciate the whole of his output adequately without the beautiful frescoes in the Vatican (happily immovable) or

the gorgeous Coronation of the Virgin in the
Louvre or such a candid and delicate work as the
National Gallery predella, originally part of his
earliest altarpiece, the badly damaged one from
San Domenico.

Fra Angelico is perhaps no longer the keepsake
idol that he still was sixty years ago. At that
time copies of little angels and others of his most
doll-like figures were so much *en vogue* that less
appreciated panels of the same date were being
cut into small bits to furnish well-seasoned wood
for them. When I had the good luck of dis-
covering the triptych by Sassetta (now in my
collection and considered as one of the great
creations of Quattrocento art) in a junkshop, I
was given to understand that such was to be its
fate. One wonders how many valuable panels
perished in that way !

But Fra Angelico's fame as a real artist, as a
great painter has grown and is more firmly
established. He has never been so deeply and
intelligently appreciated as now.

Casa al Dono
Vallombrosa
July 1955

XIX

POPULAR ART

The publication of Percy's ballads, of Mac-Pherson's *Ossian*, of Herder's *Stimmen der Voelker*, followed later by Grimm's Fairytales, Clemens Brentano's and Achim Arnim's *Des Knaben Wunderhorn* (the Boy's Cornucopia), the rediscovery of the Icelandic myths and sagas, of the German Niebelungen-Gudrun epic, of the French *Chanson de Roland* or the *Matière de Bretagne*, all prepared the way for the revolt against Malherbes Corneille and Racine, including of course their followers and imitators all over Europe. It also prepared the way for the Romantic movement with all its poses, attitudes, catchwords, battle-cries and mystiques.

Its most telling mystique was that the writings just enumerated were the spontaneous expression of this or that " folk " as a mass and not the literary products of gifted individuals, of geniuses even, acting as bards or court jesters, as jongleurs or tumblers. But " the spirit bloweth where it listeth ". Their names either never counted or were forgotten. One only may have survived and is vaguely connected with the *Chanson de Roland*, a certain Norman named Wace.

With the advance of humanization, of refinement even, with the rise of chivalry due in no small degree to one of the most gifted women in history, Eleanor of Aquitaine (wife first of Louis VI of France and then of Henry II of England), and to other great ladies, inventors of song and story began to be treated as individuals and soon came personages like Chrétien de Troyes, Gottfried of Strasburg, Wolfram of Eschenbach—to mention writers of epics only.

In the visual arts—the subject of this essay— a similar mass anonymity prevailed. Names of great prelates appear, Bernard of Hildesheim, Desiderius of Montecassino, Suger of Saint Denis. Bernard actually may have been architect and sculptor himself. Accident has preserved the album of a wandering French architect, Villard d'Hennecourt, and we know the names of a few other Frenchmen who got as far as Norway and Sweden, one of them, Etienne de Bonneuil, the architect of Upsala cathedral.

The rare names that appear in connection

with the glorious galaxy of Romanesque and Gothic cathedrals have remained hidden away in the publications of architects and no word of them has reached the public, even the cultivated public. So it was easy for the belief to impose itself that these mighty and beautiful structures grew spontaneously out of the folk soul like the great forests out of the ground. More so, if possible, with the ancillary crafts that adorned the cathedrals, abbeys, seigniorial and municipal palaces, sculpture, painting, glass, the minor arts.

After nearly seventy years of ruminating on questions of art history I am convinced that popular art is always a derivation from professional individual art, never a spontaneous upsurging from the dumb dull masses of new ways of feeling, seeing and expressing with the voice, the pen or the pencil. It may look so but on inquiry one discovers that the Anglo-Scottish ballads which seem to spring most feelingly from the suffering heart of the people were composed by highly cultivated great ladies. Mérimée, a writer as far as possible from being a mouthpiece of the masses, composed a series of " Illyrian Ballads " which nearly took in the old Goethe. The stories of Cupid and Psyche, of Hero and Leander and many other Greek hero tales find clear echoes in German and Russian popular lore.

I have never seen a specimen of popular visual art that was not a copy of a copy of a copy of something professional, classical, always suffering degradation that each copyist with the originality of incompetence introduced, until it reached the puerile, the infantile expression of the mass soul.

Folk art is to professional art what underbrush is to the forest. It flourishes where there is no professional art as in the mountain fastnesses of Central Europe and in the Balkans. In the first gifted peasants carved entertainingly naïve images, in the second needlewomen plied their craft with eminent success.

In Italy, where churches and municipalities and courts were constantly employing artists, there was poor art for poor people but scarcely any popular art. The Italian peasant was too near a town and too much under its influence to develop an art of his own. The Florentine *contadino* could afford an altarpiece by Fra Filippo which I saw sixty years ago at Bagno a Ripoli where it still stood on the altar for which it was painted (now in the Palazzo Barberini, Rome) (Plate 105). Another work of the same great Florentine (now in the Metropolitan Museum of New York) adorned the altar of a wayside chapel at Vincigliata, not a kilometre above my own house (Plate 106). A church high up on the hills above the Arno between San Giovanni and Montevarchi contains an Annunciation with predella which authoritative critics believe to be an autograph replica by Fra Angelico of the same subject now in the Prado at Madrid (Plate 107).

Of course many rustic churches and many humble folk could not afford the great artist and employed painters—mere artisans—who must have worked for very little. Not one of them whose manner cannot be traced back to the best artists of their time. The other day there turned up at an antiquarian's in Florence an altarpiece in splendid frame with predella. It represents the Madonna between Saint Simeon and Saint Thaddeus and is signed Amadeus de Pistori Pinsit (Plate 108).

The painter is a rustic imitator of a charming close follower of Benozzo Gozzoli to whom for want of a family name I have given the designation of Alunno di Benozzo. So this typical

example of popular art can be traced back to
Benozzo and through Benozzo to Fra Angelico,
etc. etc. I who have seen so many pictures in
every nook and cranny of Italy have never yet
come across a painting, no matter how crude,
how incompetent that could not be traced back
to great masters.

The same holds for sculpture and for Roman
sculpture as well. No matter whether in Rome
itself or in the rest of Italy, till the IVth century
good work remains Hellenistic and poor work
poorly imitative. I have never seen a Roman
work that had anything that would justify its
being signalled as popular in the sense of being
distinct from poor art. Indeed, I venture to
declare that from about 600 B.C. onward there
has never been in Italy a visual art that sprang
from the soil, from the heart of the masses and
was not a degradation of professional art.

Was it the same with literature, prose and
verse, folk-tales and folk-songs? I am not well
enough acquainted with the subject to have an
opinion.

In my earlier years there was scarcely a village
in the most out-of-the-way parts of Italy that
did not display one book in stationers' shops.
That book was a cheap edition of the *Reali di*

Francia. It used to be told that gondoliers in Venice would chant Ariosto and Tasso as they rowed.

And the *Stornelli* and *Rispetti* of the Pistoiese? (By the way, D'Annunzio looked amazed when I told him that to me they were real poetry.)

Perhaps the following may throw some light on the problem and furnish a fitting ending to this rambling essay. Nearly seventy years ago I knew an elderly Englishman in Rome, a Mr. Davis, who had long been a resident and lover of Italy, had published a *Voyage on the Tiber* and had the glory of being mentioned by D'Annunzio in the *Trionfo della Morte.* As a young man he was tramping on the hills high above Pistoia. It seemed to be getting too warm and he thought it might be time to turn back. He fumbled for his watch and discovered that he had not taken it with him. So he asked an old peasant who was passing what time it might be. The answer he got was : *Il calore del sole e il tocco di bronzo annunciano il mezzogiorno.* (The warmth of the sun and the resounding bell announce the noon.)

I Tatti
Settignano
February 1956

XX

THE CARRACCIS

Ewige Wiederkehr—Eternal return—of Niet-
zsche—what has been will be again and again
and again. If Cimabue held the field he will
hold it once more and again once more. Nowadays among *les Jeunes* it is he, not Giotto, who has
applause—*il grido*.

When I first came to Italy nearly seventy years
ago it was Carlo Dolci, it was Domenichino, it
was Guido Reni who really spoke to Italians and
tourists, although of course *il Divino Raffaello*
remained enthroned and all but inaccessible, high
up in the Empyrean. I cannot recall that at
that time the Carraccis came in for the loving
admiration now bestowed on them. But it was
the Carraccis who held the field for generations
and particularly at the beginning of the XIXth
century. In 1803 or soon after that date the
Orléans Collection offered for sale in London was
bought by a group of two or three noblemen.

They were to draw lots as to who should have the first choice, and although there were marvellous Titians to choose from it was understood as a matter of course that the privileged one would take a small Carracci considered to be the supreme jewel of the collection.

Relatively ignored for a century as favourites, the Carraccis are now returning with drums and trumpets, and as is fit they make their *grande entrée* in Bologna, their home town.

In the hall and corridors of the Archiginnasio are collected works from everywhere, from all continents and from the isles of the sea. Even the National Gallery of London for the first time in generations has lent some of its treasures.

The paintings are shown, given the available space, in a way that could scarcely be surpassed, and the drawings in exemplary fashion. We owe much to the knowledge, the experience and the zest of Professor Gnudi, of Dottor Cavalli and of their staff, as well as to Mr. Denis Mahon. In the noble yet quaint Anatomical Hall and in the spacious corridors Mr. Mahon offers a perfect object-lesson of how drawings should be displayed. All should come and see how it can be done. A real *trouvaille* is the placing of reproductions of

the finished works along with the studies made
for them.

Add that the catalogue contains not only guid-
ing appreciation but the detailed annals of the
Carraccis' careers and a bibliography of stagger-
ing proportions. A treasure of basic facts to aid
understanding. Each generation will interpret
them according to its own whims and passions.

In short, one could not do more than has been
done here to attract and interest.

With what results ?

Almost none for me who have enjoyed seventy
years of experience, gustation, appreciation,
enjoyment of the whole world's visual art from
Paleolithic artifacts down to the great achievements of the nineteenth century. Little has
escaped my zestful curiosity. Nor have I been
unaware of the Carraccis. Scores upon scores
of times have I spent hours gazing at the frescoes
in the Palazzo Farnese (Plate 109), and their
paintings in the gallery and in the churches of
Bologna are well known to me. I never thought
of them as among the Great Artists or as worthy
of *aesthetical* as distinct from historical interest.

Of course " the labourer " as the gospel tells
" is worthy of his hire ", and it is natural that
scholars who have concentrated their attention,

zeal and ardour on organizing this exemplary show of the Carraccis should not retain towards them a sense of proportion like mine. I am ready to admit much that is admirable in single works. I applaud the Carraccis for returning to sanity from the " Mannerist debauch ", for respecting the human figure made in God's image and not treating it as Procrustes did, pulling it out to fill their concepts. I strongly enjoy the glimpses of distant horizons even in their, to me, most unattractive altarpieces. On the other hand, I cannot stomach their lack of proportion, between one figure and the other their false religious sentiment, their pedantry, their conventional and relatively lifeless drawing and no less conventional painting.

I shall not try to distinguish one of the brothers from the others. They form a group with the same visual and manual habits, the same ideas and ideals. The differences are only the inevitable ones existing between one object and another, even between machine-made ones. By infecting each other the brothers evened out what innate differences there may have been between them.

Rather than insist on negation, let me draw attention to a few pictures that have given me pleasure, aroused my interest or even my

E.A.—L

admiration. Also let me add that while scarcely more than has been done could be done with pictures and drawings, the most significant work of the Carraccis was mural. Although photographs and even projections of colour slides do their best to make up for their absence, yet that absence should always be kept in mind.

Once in a while they attract as illustration and interest as innovation. To me the most compelling work exhibited is the *Butcher's Shop* from Christ Church, Oxford (Plate 110). It is admirably composed and seen at due distance each person, each object holds its place. Yet it is not that which excites my curiosity. Rather its realism. I cannot recall movement, gesture, expression as " true to life ", painted earlier or indeed for a long time later. It went with other treasured paintings from Mantua to England. One wonders what the Gonzagas, what Charles I and their courtiers thought of it. Compare the carcass here with Rembrandt's in the Louvre. Rembrandt does not paint anything he does not see, whereas Annibale Carracci paints every vertebra in the spine of the carcass because he knows it is there. The great Hollander ignores what he knows and represents only what he sees while viewing the composition as a whole. Did

Velasquez know this picture? One is tempted to believe that it was lingering in his memory when he composed his Don Juan, so like the soldier in the *Butcher's Shop* fumbling for coins. (How valuable it would be by the way to have a full detailed account of Velasquez' two visits to Italy, where he went, what he saw and what effect it had on his career.)

For sheer geniality of painting and as a representation of a difficult subject, without sentimentality and with none of the usual Carraccesque exaggerations, I recommend the *Martyrdom* of *Sant' Angelo* from the Bologna picture gallery (Plate 111).

The head of a youth covered with a peaked felt hat and wide flaps over the ears from the Capitoline Pinacoteca (Plate 112) just misses being nearly as good as a Vermeer Van Delft, and when in better condition must have been even nearer to him.

I enjoyed greatly the Holy Family crossing the Nile from Casa Tacconi in Bologna, the billowing sail, the gondolier, the cosy personages ; as in the paintings of the Nazarener school of the early XIXth century (Plate 113). The Carraccis seem to have lost no occasion for introducing gondoliers into their pictures.

Interesting is a composition of female nudes from the Vienna Gallery with a cupid in the foreground, catalogued as *Love in Lethe (Amor Letheo)*, so Tintorettesque that it could have easily been attributed to the over-powering Venetian (Plate 114). I have already mentioned the pleasure I derived from glimpses of distant horizons. Best of all the compositions where landscape dominates, as in the Roman scene with a broken bridge and distant mountains from Berlin (Plate 115), or in the Doria Lunette with the small figures of the Holy Family in the foreground (Plate 116), or in the Saint Eustace with the stag from the Naples Pinacoteca (Plate 117). They all are pictures of scenery rather than efforts to reproduce nature as Cézanne and his followers have tried it. I venture to ask which is the more enjoyable?

All in all, what I carry away from this exemplary exhibition is the Catalogue of the Paintings with its extensive information about the Carraccis and its sensitive appreciation and interpretation of every work exhibited.

I Tatti
Settignano
October 1956

GENERAL INDEX

156

Giovanni di Francesco, 30 note,
Giusto di Andrea, 29, 36
Glasgow, Art Gallery, 45, 100,
116
Glennew, Kentucky, 26
Gnudi, Cesare, 118, 149
Goethe, 71, 144
Goettingen, Museum, 33
Goldsmith, Oliver, 96
Gongora, 77
Gozzoli, Benozzo, 21, 24, 26,
31, 145
Guardi, Francesco, 4
Guggenheim Collection, 64

Heine, Heinrich, 92

John, Augustus, 19

Kairouan, Great Mosque at,
137

Landscape, romantic, 154
— Tuscan, 135–136
Laurencin, Marie, 73
Lawrence, Sir Thomas, 15
Lendinara, Duomo, 51, 52
Leningrad, Hermitage, 100,
109, 111–115, 116
Leonardo da Vinci, 67–72, 95,
96, 100, 135
Lessing, Gotthold Ephraim, 83
Liebermann, Max, 99
Lippi, Filippino, 30
Lippi, Fra Filippo, 26, 31–36,
32 note, 37, 137, 144
Lombard, Lambert, 88

London, British Museum, 21,
27
— Christie Sale 1923, 121
— Courtauld Institute, 25
— Livijn Collection, 37
— National Gallery, 24, 48, 67,
114, 115, 121, 140, 149
— Orléans Sale 1803, 148
— Royal Academy, Exhibitions at, 17
Lyons, Aynard Collection, 36
— Museum, 25

Machiavelli, Zanobi, 29–38
Madrid, Prado, 46, 88, 138,
145
— Royal Palace, 63
Mahon, Denis, 120, 149
Manierism, 151
Manuscripts, illuminated, 21–28, 78–86
Massa Marittima, Museum,
40
Master of San Miniato, 24, 26,
27, 28, 29, 30
Master of the Carrand Triptych, 30, 30 note, 33
Master of the Castello Nativity,
30, 33
Matisse, Henri, 128–133
Mérimée, Prosper, 143
Meyer, Eduard, 83
Michelangelo, 64, 71, 94, 106
Milan, Picasso Exhibition 1953,
72–77
— Santa Maria delle Grazie,
67–71
Molmenti, Pompeo, 57, 61

E.A.—L*

LIST OF PLATES

11 Giusto di Andrea (?) : Pope Clement IV or V. (*Print Room, British Museum, London.*)

12 Zanobi Machiavelli : Madonna—formerly Hurd Collection. (*Fine Arts Museum, Richmond, Virginia.*)

13 Zanobi Machiavelli : Madonna. (*S. Andrea a Bottinaccio, Environs of Florence.*)

14 Zanobi Machiavelli : Madonna. (*Park Bennet Sale, New York.*)

15 Master of the Castello Nativity : Madonna. (*Museum, Göttingen.*)

16 Zanobi Machiavelli : Madonna. (*Accademia Carrara, Bergamo.*)

17 Zanobi Machiavelli : " Modello " for Altarpiece. (*Condé Museum, Chantilly.*)

18 Zanobi Machiavelli : Portable Altar. (*Walters Museum, Baltimore.*)

19 Zanobi Machiavelli : Annunciation. (*S. Martino a Mensola, Environs of Florence.*)

20 Zanobi Machiavelli : Madonna. (*Museum, Besançon.*)

21 Zanobi Machiavelli : Madonna and Angels. (*Yale University Museum, New Haven, Conn.*)

22 Zanobi Machiavelli : Madonna with Saints and Donors. (*Formerly Livijn Collection, London.*)

23 Simone Martini : Miracles of the Blessed Agostino Novello. (*Sant' Agostino, Siena.*)

24 Carlo Crivelli : Saint Catherine. (*National Gallery, London.*)

25 Venetian School around 1540 : Adoration of the Magi. (*National Gallery, Dublin.*)

26 Andrea Delitio : Nativity of the Virgin. (*Duomo, Atri.*)

27 Domenico Mancini (?) : " Sacra Conversazione." (*Louvre, Paris.*)

28 Giovanni Cariani : Idyll. (*Accademia Carrara, Bergamo.*)

29 Titian : Miracle of St. Anthony of Padua. (*Scuola del Santo, Padua.*)

30 Domenico Mancini : Madonna Enthroned. (*Duomo, Lendinara.*)

31 Domenico Mancini : Angel (detail). (*Duomo, Lendinara.*)

32 Domenico Mancini (?) : Head of St. Sebastian (detail). (*Louvre, Paris.*)

33 Domenico Mancini : Bust of Youth. (*Borghese Gallery, Rome.*)

34   Contemporary copy of the " Sacra Conversazi-
     one " in the Louvre.   (*Formerly Farrer Collection,
     London.*)

35   Domenico Mancini (?) : Thomiris with Head of
     Cirus.   (*Formerly Mallman Collection.*)

36   Domenico Mancini (?) : Lute Player and
     Cavalier.   (*Formerly Scarpa Collection, Motta di
     Livenza.*)

37   Domenico Mancini : Madonna with Two Saints.
     (*Carlo Gamba Collection, Florence.*)

38   Domenico Mancini (?) : Christ and the
     Adulteress.   (*Condé Museum, Chantilly.*)

39   G. B. Tiepolo : Ceiling panel.   (*Contini Bonacossi
     Collection, Florence.*)

40   G. B. Tiepolo : " Bozzetto " for one of the
     Madrid ceilings.   (*National Gallery, Washing-
     ton.*)

41   G. B. Tiepolo : " Bozzetto " for a Martyrdom of
     Saint Sebastian.   (*Museum of Art, Cleveland,
     Ohio.*)

42   G. B. Tiepolo : The Sacrifice of Ifigenia.
     (*Wedells Collection, Hamburg.*)

43   G. B. Tiepolo : " Madonna del Cardellino."
     (*National Gallery, Washington.*)

44   G. B. Tiepolo : Sketch for a Flight into Egypt. (*Museum of Art, Cleveland, Ohio.*)

45   G. B. Tiepolo : Banquet of Anthony and Cleopatra — formerly in the Hermitage. (*National Gallery, Melbourne.*)

46   G. B. Tiepolo : Triumph of Anfitrite. (*Picture Gallery, Dresden.*)

47   G. B. Tiepolo : Rinaldo and Armida. (*Dahlem Museum, Berlin.*)

48   Leonardo da Vinci : Last Supper (before the Restoration). (*S. Maria delle Grazie, Milan.*)

49   Mauro Pelliccioli while explaining the restoration of the Last Supper to Bernard Berenson.

50   Leonardo da Vinci : Last Supper (after Restoration). (*S. Maria delle Grazie, Milan.*)

51   Pablo Picasso : The artist's son, aged two—1923.

52   Marie Laurencin : Harlequin. (*Vogel Collection, Philadelphia.*)

53   Pablo Picasso : The Artist's Mother—1923.

54   Pablo Picasso : Woman dressed in a Shirt— 1921. (*Eichmann Collection, Zürich.*)

55   Pablo Picasso : Seated Woman—1937-38.

56   Pablo Picasso : Seated Woman (1937–38).

57   Pablo Picasso : Owls (Ceramic).

58   Pablo Picasso : A coq. (*Illustration to Buffon's Histoire Naturelle.*)

59   Pablo Picasso : Centaurs Fighting. (Ceramic).

60   Pablo Picasso : Woman at the Mirror. (Ceramic.)

61   Christ in Glory—Exultet Roll of the XIth century. (*Episcopal Palace, Bari.*)

62   Adam and Eve—Exultet Roll of the XIIIth century. (*Museum, Pisa.*)

63   Easter Candlestick. (*San Paolo fuori le mura, Rome.*)

64   Christ's Entry into Jerusalem. (*From the Codex Purpureus Rossanensis. VIth century. Archbishop's Palace, Rossano.*)

65   Domenico Caprioli (?) : The Flautist. (*Borghese Gallery, Rome.*)

66   Domenico Caprioli (?) : The Singer. (*Borghese Gallery, Rome.*)

67   Giorgione : The Old Woman " Col Tempo ". (*Accademia, Venice.*)

68   Giorgione : The Gypsy Woman (Detail of the " Tempesta "). (*Accademia, Venice.*)

69 Giovanni Cariani (?) : Madonna (*Ashmolean Museum, Oxford.*)

70 Giovanni Cariani (?) : Madonna. (*Hermitage Museum, Leningrad.*)

71 Giovanni Cariani (?) : Madonna with Two Saints. (*Accademia, Venice.*)

72 Giovanni Cariani (?) : Madonna. (*Viezzoli Collection, Genoa.*)

73 Giovanni Cariani : Madonna. (*National Gallery, London.*)

74 Giovanni Cariani : Madonna with St. Elizabeth and the Two Children. (*National Gallery, Palazzo Barberini, Rome.*)

75 Giovanni Cariani : Invention of the Cross. (*Accademia Carrara, Bergamo.*)

76 Guido Reni : Massacre of the Innocents. (*Picture Gallery, Bologna.*)

77 Guido Reni : Samson. (*Picture Gallery, Bologna.*)

78 Guido Reni : The Archangel Michael. (*Cappuccini Church, Rome.*)

79 Guido Reni : Giving of the Keys to St. Peter. (*Museum, Perpignan.*)

80 Guido Reni : John the Baptist. (*Dulwich College, London.*)

81 Guido Reni : Meeting of Christ and John the Baptist. (*Picture Gallery of the Girolamini, Naples.*)

82 Guido Reni : Portrait of a Pope. (*Methuen Collection, Corsham Court.*)

83 Guido Reni : Portrait of a Cardinal. (*Formerly Wimborne Collection, Canford Manor.*)

84 Guido Reni : Bust of Old Woman. (*Picture Gallery, Bologna.*)

85 Guido Reni : So-called Portrait of his Mother. (*Picture Gallery, Bologna.*)

86 Guido Reni : Bust of Old Man. (*Formerly Erskine Collection, Scotland.*)

87 Follower of Jacopo Bellini, towards 1460 : Scenes of the Passion (detail). (*Cini Collection, Monselice.*)

88 Follower of Jacopo Bellini, towards 1460 : Scenes of the Passion (monochrome). (*Cini Collection, Monselice.*)

89 Monsu' Desiderio : The Anointing of King Saul. (*Private Collection, Rome.*)

90 Venetian towards 1460 : Adoration of the Magi (monochrome). (*Cini Collection, Monselice.*)

91 Venetian towards 1460 : Adoration of the Magi (detail). (*Cini Collection, Monselice.*)

92 Venetian towards 1460 : Adoration of the Magi (detail). (*Cini Collection, Monselice.*)

93 Matisse : Nudes Dancing. (*Museum of Modern Art, Moscow.*)

94 Antonio Pollaiuolo : Nudes Dancing. (*Torre del Gallo, Arcetri.*)

95 Matisse : Flowering Meadow and Trees. (*Museum, Belgrade—formerly Berenson Collection.*)

96 Matisse : Virgin with Child (sketch). (*Chapel of Vence.*)

97 A, B Walls of the Grand Mosque of Kairouan.

98 Fra Angelico : Pietà. (*S. Marco Museum, Florence.*)

99 Fra Angelico : View of Jerusalem (detail of the great Deposition). (*S. Marco Museum, Florence.*)

100 Fra Angelico : Madonna with Eight Saints—1438. (*S. Marco Museum, Florence.*)

101 Fra Angelico : Sposalizio and Visitation. (*Diocesan Museum, Cortona.*)

102 Fra Angelico : Presentation of Christ in the Temple and Dormition of the Virgin. (*Diocesan Museum, Cortona.*)

103 Fra Angelico : Saints and Blessed—detail of the Coronation. (*S. Marco Museum, Florence.*)

104 Library of San Marco : after restoration.

105 Fra Filippo Lippi : Annunciation. (*National Gallery, Barberini Palace, Rome.*)

106   Fra Filippo Lippi : Alessandri Triptych. (*Metropolitan Museum, New York.*)

107   Fra Angelico (studio) : Annunciation. (*Montecarlo, Valdarno Superiore.*)

108   Amedeo da Pistoia : Madonna with Two Saints. (*Private Collection, Florence.*)

109   Annibale and Agostino Carracci : The God Pan and Diana (fresco). (*Farnese Palace, Rome.*)

110   Annibale Carracci : The Butcher's Shop. (*Christchurch, Oxford.*)

111   Lodovico Carracci : Martyrdom of S. Angelo. (*Picture Gallery, Bologna.*)

112   Lodovico Carracci : Bust of Youth with Pointed Hat. (*Capitoline Picture Gallery, Rome.*)

113   Agostino Carracci : Flight into Egypt. (*Casa Tacconi, Bologna.*)

114   Agostino Carracci : " L'Amor Letheo." (*Picture Gallery, Vienna.*)

115   Annibale Carracci : Roman Landscape. (*Dahlem Museum, Berlin.*)

116   Annibale Carracci : Flight into Egypt. (*Doria Gallery, Rome.*)

117   Annibale Carracci : The Vision of St. Eustache (*Picture Gallery, Naples.*)

ILLUSTRATIONS

1

ATTRIBUTED TO ANNIBALE CARRACCI: VIEW OF THE OLD CENTRE OF FLORENCE.
PRIVATE COLLECTION, PARIS.

2

BERNARDO BELLOTTO: VIEW OF THE PONTE VECCHIO.   MUSEUM OF FINE ARTS, BOSTON.

3

VIEW OF THE LUNGARNO ACCIAIOLI BEFORE 1944.

4

VIEW OF THE PONTE VECCHIO BEFORE 1944.

5

6

Post lunā ascēdit mars sanctes sanguinē baptismalē ascēdit aut returriī avalutissi
mum soluum qui soluum clarissimū offuscabit ai lilio zeruce aquila cruciabit mini
me edificabit michi templū qui uir sāguinū es celo i moezaro uirtute simulata zc
nigramis dissipans supstlua solus pacem cohartans renozans uniuersa : ~

7

8

9

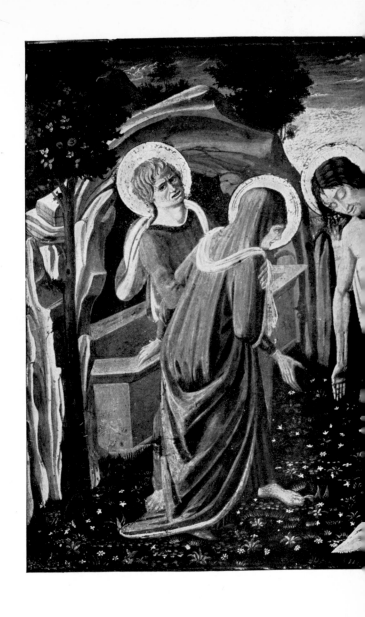

10

MASTER OF SAN MINIATO: DEPOSITION.   MUSEUM, LYONS.

11

GIUSTO DI ANDREA (?): POPE CLEMENT IV OR V.
PRINT ROOM, BRITISH MUSEUM, LONDON.

12

ZANOBI MACHIAVELLI: MADONNA. FORMERLY HURD COLLECTION.
FINE ARTS MUSEUM, RICHMOND, VIRGINIA.

13

ZANOBI MACHIAVELLI: MADONNA. S. ANDREA A BOTTINACCIO, ENVIRONS OF FLORENCE.

14

ZANOBI MACHIAVELLI: MADONNA.   PARK BENNET SALE, NEW YORK.

15

MASTER OF THE CASTELLO NATIVITY: MADONNA.   MUSEUM, GÖTTINGEN.

16

ZANOBI MACHIAVELLI: MADONNA. ACCADEMIA CARRARA, BERGAMO.

17

ZANOBI MACHIAVELLI: "MODELLO" FOR ALTARPIECE.   CONDÉ MUSEUM, CHANTILLY.

18

ZANOBI MACHIAVELLI: PORTABLE ALTAR.   WALTERS MUSEUM, BALTIMORE.

19

ZANOBI MACHIAVELLI: ANNUNCIATION.   S. MARTINO A MENSOLA, ENVIRONS OF FLORENCE.

20

ZANOBI MACHIAVELLI: MADONNA. MUSEUM, BESANÇON.

21

ZANOBI MACHIAVELLI: MADONNA AND ANGELS.
YALE UNIVERSITY MUSEUM, NEW HAVEN, CONN.

22

ZANOBI MACHIAVELLI: MADONNA WITH SAINTS AND DONORS.
FORMERLY LIVIJN COLLECTION, LONDON.

23

SIMONE MARTINI: MIRACLES OF THE BLESSED AGOSTINO NOVELLO. SANT' AGOSTINO, SIENA.

24

CARLO CRIVELLI: SAINT CATHERINE.   NATIONAL GALLERY, LONDON.

VENETIAN SCHOOL AROUND 1540: ADORATION OF THE MAGI. NATIONAL GALLERY, DUBLIN.

26

ANDREA DELITIO: NATIVITY OF THE VIRGIN.   DUOMO, ATRI.

27

DOMENICO MANCINI (?): "SACRA CONVERSAZIONE." LOUVRE, PARIS.

28

GIOVANNI CARIANI: IDYLL.   ACCADEMIA CARRARA, BERGAMO.

29

TITIAN: MIRACLE OF ST. ANTHONY OF PADUA.   SCUOLA DEL SANTO, PADUA.

30

DOMENICO MANCINI: MADONNA ENTHRONED. DUOMO, LENDINARA.

31

DOMENICO MANCINI: ANGEL (DETAIL). DUOMO, LENDINARA.

32

DOMENICO MANCINI(?) HEAD OF ST. SEBASTIAN (DETAIL).   LOUVRE, PARIS.

33

DOMENICO MANCINI: BUST OF YOUTH.   BORGHESE GALLERY, ROME.

34

CONTEMPORARY COPY OF THE " SACRA CONVERSAZIONE " IN THE LOUVRE.
FORMERLY FARRER COLLECTION, LONDON.

35

DOMENICO MANCINI (?): THOMIRIS WITH HEAD OF CIRUS.
FORMERLY MALLMAN COLLECTION.

37
DOMENICO MANCINI: MADONNA WITH TWO SAINTS.
CARLO GAMBA COLLECTION, FLORENCE.

38

DOMENICO MANCINI (?): CHRIST AND THE ADULTERESS. CONDÉ MUSEUM, CHANTILLY.

39

G. B. TIEPOLO: CEILING PANEL.   CONTINI BONACOSSI COLLECTION, FLORENCE.

40

G. B. TIEPOLO: "BOZZETTO" FOR ONE OF THE MADRID CEILINGS.
NATIONAL GALLERY, WASHINGTON.

41

G. B. TIEPOLO: " BOZZETTO " FOR A MARTYRDOM OF SAINT SEBASTIAN.
MUSEUM OF ART, CLEVELAND, OHIO.

42

G. B. TIEPOLO: THE SACRIFICE OF IFIGENIA.   WEDELLS COLLECTION, HAMBURG.

43

G. B. TIÉPOLO: " MADONNA DEL CARDELLINO." NATIONAL GALLERY, WASHINGTON.

44
G. B. TIEPOLO: SKETCH FOR A FLIGHT INTO EGYPT.
MUSEUM OF ART, CLEVELAND, OHIO.

45

G. B. TIEPOLO: BANQUET OF ANTHONY AND CLEOPATRA.
FORMERLY IN THE HERMITAGE. NATIONAL GALLERY, MELBOURNE.

G. B. TIEPOLO: TRIUMPH OF ANFITRITE. PICTURE GALLERY, DRESDEN.

47

G. B. TIEPOLO: RINALDO AND ARMIDA.   DAHLEM MUSEUM, BERLIN.

49

MAURO PELLICCIOLI WHILE EXPLAINING THE RESTORATION OF THE LAST SUPPER TO BERNARD BERENSON.

48

LEONARDO DA VINCI: LAST SUPPER (BEFORE THE RESTORATION). S. MARIA DELLE GRAZIE, MILAN

LEONARDO DA VINCI: LAST SUPPER (AFTER RESTORATION). S. MARIA DELLE GRAZIE, MILAN.

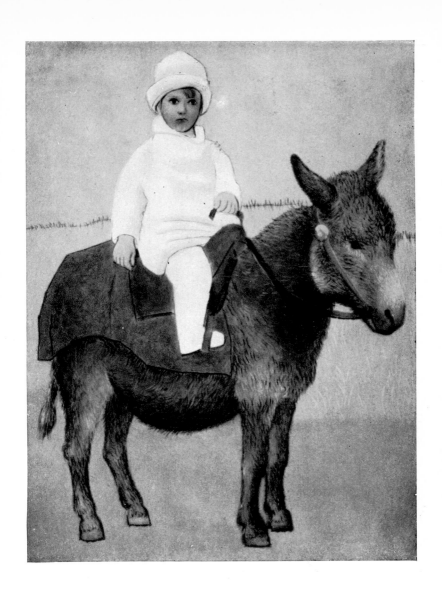

51

PABLO PICASSO: THE ARTIST'S SON, AGED TWO (1923).

52

MARIE LAURENCIN: HARLEQUIN.　VOGEL COLLECTION, PHILADELPHIA.

53

PABLO PICASSO: THE ARTIST'S MOTHER (1923).

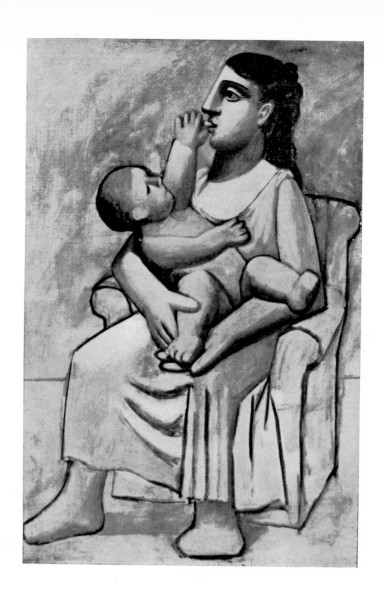

54

PABLO PICASSO: WOMAN DRESSED IN A SHIRT (1921). EICHMANN COLLECTION, ZÜRICH.

55

PABLO PICASSO: SEATED WOMAN (1937/38).

56

PABLO PICASSO: SEATED WOMAN (1937/38).

57

PABLO PICASSO: OWLS (CERAMIC).

58

PABLO PICASSO: A COQ (ILLUSTRATION TO BUFFON'S HISTOIRE NATURELLE).

59

PABLO PICASSO: CENTAURS FIGHTING (CERAMIC).

60

PABLO PICASSO: WOMAN AT THE MIRROR (CERAMIC).

61

CHRIST IN GLORY.   EXULTET ROLL OF THE XITH CENTURY.   EPISCOPAL PALACE, BARI.

62

ADAM AND EVE.   EXULTET ROLL OF THE XIIITH CENTURY.   MUSEUM, PISA.

63

EASTER CANDLESTICK.   SAN PAOLO FUORI LE MURA, ROME.

64

CHRIST'S ENTRY INTO JERUSALEM.   FROM THE CODEX PURPUREUS ROSSANENSIS.   VITH CENTURY.
ARCHBISHOP'S PALACE, ROSSANO.

65

DOMENICO CAPRIOLI (?): THE FLAUTIST
BORGHESE GALLERY, ROME.

66

DOMENICO CAPRIOLI (?): THE SINGER.   BORGHESE GALLERY, ROME.

67

GIORGIONE: THE OLD WOMAN " COL TEMPO ".   ACCADEMIA, VENICE.

68

GIORGIONE: THE GYPSY WOMAN (DETAIL OF THE " TEMPESTA "). ACCADEMIA, VENICE.

69

GIOVANNI CARIANI (?): MADONNA.   ASHMOLEAN MUSEUM, OXFORD.

70

GIOVANNI CARIANI (?): MADONNA. HERMITAGE MUSEUM, LENINGRAD.

71

GIOVANNI CARIANI (?): MADONNA WITH TWO SAINTS.
ACCADEMIA, VENICE.

72

GIOVANNI CARIANI (?): MADONNA.   VIEZZOLI COLLECTION, GENOA.

73

GIOVANNI CARIANI: MADONNA.   NATIONAL GALLERY, LONDON.

74

GIOVANNI CARIANI: MADONNA WITH ST. ELIZABETH AND THE TWO CHILDREN.
NATIONAL GALLERY, PALAZZO BARBERINI, ROME.

75

GIOVANNI CARIANI: INVENTION OF THE CROSS.
ACCADEMIA CARRARA, BERGAMO.

76

GUIDO RENI: MASSACRE OF THE INNOCENTS.   PICTURE GALLERY, BOLOGNA.

77

GUIDO RENI: SAMSON. PICTURE GALLERY, BOLOGNA.

78

GUIDO RENI: THE ARCHANGEL MICHAEL. CAPPUCCINI CHURCH, ROME.

79

GUIDO RENI: GIVING OF THE KEYS TO ST. PETER. MUSEUM, PERPIGNAN.

80

GUIDO RENI: JOHN THE BAPTIST.
DULWICH COLLEGE, LONDON.

81

GUIDO RENI: MEETING OF CHRIST AND JOHN THE BAPTIST.
PICTURE GALLERY OF THE GIROLAMINI, NAPLES.

82

GUIDO RENI: PORTRAIT OF A POPE.   METHUEN COLLECTION, CORSHAM COURT.

83

GUIDO RENI: PORTRAIT OF A CARDINAL.   FORMERLY WIMBORNE COLLECTION, CANFORD MANOR.

84

GUIDO RENI: BUST OF OLD WOMAN.   PICTURE GALLERY, BOLOGNA.

85

GUIDO RENI: SO-CALLED PORTRAIT OF HIS MOTHER. PICTURE GALLERY, BOLOGNA.

86
GUIDO RENI: BUST OF OLD MAN.
FORMERLY ERSKINE COLLECTION, SCOTLAND.

87

FOLLOWER OF JACOPO BELLINI, TOWARDS 1460: SCENES OF THE PASSION (DETAIL).
CINI COLLECTION, MONSELICE.

88

FOLLOWER OF JACOPO BELLINI, TOWARDS 1460: SCENES OF THE PASSION (MONOCHROME).
CINI COLLECTION, MONSELICE.

89

MONSU' DESIDERIO: THE ANOINTING OF KING SAUL.
PRIVATE COLLECTION, ROME.

90

VENETIAN TOWARDS 1460: ADORATION OF THE MAGI (MONOCHROME).
CINI COLLECTION, MONSELICE.

91

VENETIAN TOWARDS 1460: ADORATION OF THE MAGI (DETAIL).
CINI COLLECTION, MONSELICE.

92

VENETIAN TOWARDS 1460: ADORATION OF THE MAGI (DETAIL).
CINI COLLECTION, MONSELICE.

93
MATISSE: NUDES DANCING.
MUSEUM OF MODERN ART, MOSCOW.

94

ANTONIO POLLAIUOLO: NUDES DANCING.
TORRE DEL GALLO, ARCETRI.

95

MATISSE: FLOWERING MEADOW AND TREES.
MUSEUM, BELGRADE (FORMERLY BERENSON COLLECTION).

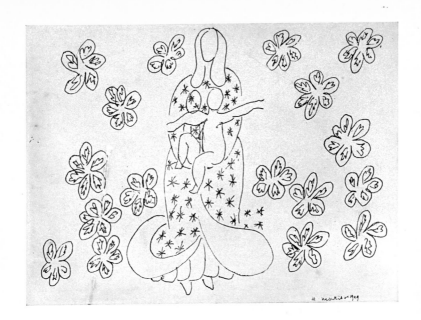

96

MATISSE: VIRGIN WITH CHILD (SKETCH).
CHAPEL OF VENCE.

A

B

97 A, B
WALLS OF THE GRAND MOSQUE OF KAIROUAN.

98

FRA ANGELICO: PIETÀ.   S. MARCO MUSEUM, FLORENCE.

99

FRA ANGELICO: VIEW OF JERUSALEM (DETAIL OF THE GREAT DEPOSITION).
S. MARCO MUSEUM, FLORENCE.

100

FRA ANGELICO: MADONNA WITH EIGHT SAINTS—1438.
S. MARCO MUSEUM, FLORENCE.

101

102

FRA ANGELICO: PRESENTATION OF CHRIST IN THE TEMPLE AND DORMITION OF THE VIRGIN.
DIOCESAN MUSEUM, CORTONA.

FRA ANGELICO: SAINTS AND BLESSED—DETAIL OF THE CORONATION.
S. MARCO MUSEUM, FLORENCE.

104

LIBRARY OF SAN MARCO (AFTER RESTORATION).

105

FRA FILIPPO LIPPI: ANNUNCIATION. NATIONAL GALLERY, BARBERINI PALACE, ROME.

106

FRA FILIPPO LIPPI: ALESSANDRI TRIPTYCH.   METROPOLITAN MUSEUM, NEW YORK.

107

FRA ANGELICO (STUDIO): ANNUNCIATION.
MONTE CARLO, VALDARNO SUPERIORE.

108

AMEDEO DA PISTOIA: MADONNA WITH TWO SAINTS.
PRIVATE COLLECTION, FLORENCE.

109

ANNIBALE AND AGOSTINO CARRACCI: THE GOD PAN AND DIANA (FRESCO).
FARNESE PALACE, ROME.

110
ANNIBALE CARRACCI: THE BUTCHER'S SHOP.
CHRISTCHURCH, OXFORD.

111

LODOVICO CARRACCI: MARTYRDOM OF S. ANGELO.
PICTURE GALLERY, BOLOGNA.

112

LODOVICO CARRACCI: BUST OF YOUTH WITH POINTED HAT.
CAPITOLINE PICTURE GALLERY, ROME.

113

114

AGOSTINO CARRACCI: " L'AMOR LETHEO." PICTURE GALLERY, VIENNA.

115

ANNIBALE CARRACCI: ROMAN LANDSCAPE. DAHLEM MUSEUM, BERLIN.

116

ANNIBALE CARRACCI: FLIGHT INTO EGYPT.   DORIA GALLERY, ROME.

117

ANNIBALE CARRACCI: THE VISION OF ST. EUSTACHE.
PICTURE GALLERY, NAPLES.